SHADOWS
IN THE
STEAM

SHADOWS
IN THE
STEAM

THE HAUNTED
RAILWAYS OF BRITAIN

DAVID BRANDON & ALAN BROOKE

The
History
Press

First published 2009
This edition 2011

The History Press
The Mill, Brimscombe Port
Stroud, Gloucestershire, GL5 2QG
www.thehistorypress.co.uk

British Library Cataloguing in Publication Data.
A catalogue record for this book is available from the British Library.

ISBN 978 0 7524 6184 7

Typesetting and origination by The History Press
Printed in Great Britain

Manufacturing managed by Jellyfish Print Solutions Ltd

CONTENTS

Introduction: Ghosts and Spooky Spectres

'Millions of Spiritual Creatures walk the Earth
Unseen, both when we wake and when we sleep.'

John Milton, *Paradise Lost*, Book IV

The ultimate mystery of life is what happens to us when we die. Is the vital spark, the soul that makes each of us unique individuals, simply snuffed out to be followed rapidly by the decay of our physical parts? Most of us are uncomfortable with the idea that the world with which we are so familiar continues after we die and, in particular, that it will cope perfectly well without us. How much better to hope or believe that there is indeed an afterlife? Such a possibility is, however, viewed by most of us with a mixture of awe, trepidation and downright fear.

Many of the world's religions are preoccupied with the question of the continued existence of our souls after physical death. Indeed some religions teach that the earthly life is merely a preparation for the next, and that, when we die, we will have to account to the Deity for what we have done with our lives. Such religions have created elaborate codes of rights and wrongs which we ignore literally at our peril.

Most religions have created destinations for the souls of the departed. In the case of Christianity this is Heaven, the place where the righteous and good go and enjoy an idyllic existence for ever-after, and Hell, a state of perpetual nastiness for those who have devoted themselves to a life of sin. Some Christians believe in a third destination known as Purgatory. This is where souls undertake a process of being tried and tested until a decision is reached as to whether they should be elevated to Heaven or consigned to Hell.

If it is believed that human souls live on after the death of their material parts, it is only a small step to visualise the dead returning to the world of the living under certain circumstances. In many cultures it is thought that the dead yearn to return to the scene of their earthly lives and that they bitterly resent and envy those who they left behind who are still alive. The soul therefore returns, often angry and seeking revenge on someone who it perhaps believed wronged it while it was still alive. If, for example, its life was ended by murder, perhaps it wants to settle the hash of the murderer. There may be all sorts of other reasons why it wants to make its feelings known to the still-living.

On occasions the soul is apparently a trifle confused, but it appears to want to sort out some things that were left unresolved or otherwise unsatisfactory when its owner died. Perhaps it objects to the manner and place of its burial. Equally the soul may return if its physical remains are disturbed or treated with a lack of respect. It may return to provide someone living with a warning concerning their behaviour or perhaps to tell them of an impending disaster. A prime time for a ghostly reappearance in the land of the living is on the anniversary of a person's death. Again, if any of this is to be believed, the ghost sometimes returns out of curiosity, simply to check on how affairs are being conducted in its absence. Some ghosts seem intent on returning to resume the habitual activities they undertook while still alive. Yet others act as if they want to seek atonement for the sins they committed while they were living. When it manifests itself on its return, the soul is said to be a ghost. Manifestations attributed to ghosts have both fascinated and frightened humans since the dawn of mankind.

There are many ways in which ghosts make themselves known. They may be seen or heard, although more often people claim that they have 'sensed' their activity or presence rather than anything more tangible. Perhaps they have smelt the stench of bodily corruption or experienced a sudden and literally chilling fall in the temperature around them. Unexplained footfalls; items removed or rearranged without apparent human agency; disembodied sighs, cries and groans; things that go bump in the night. Some people claim to have caught images of paranormal entities or activity on film, but the authenticity of such images is often disputed.

All these and a host of other unexplained phenomena feature in the continuous flow of reports made by people who claim to have had encounters with ghosts or other supernatural phenomena. Many of these people are not naturally suggestible, are not attention-seekers and may even be positively stolid and unimaginative. Some were frankly sceptical about anything to do with the paranormal before they had such an experience. In most circles a person talking about seeing ghosts is likely to invite ridicule. Being the butt of mockery makes most people feel uncomfortable. For this reason it is likely that many unexplained phenomena go unreported and therefore unpublicised.

Some of the following stories are of what might be called 'serial hauntings', where apparently the same ghostly activity is repeated in or around the same place. Other activities seem to be more of a one-off. Perhaps the ghost has completed the purpose for which it came back and, having no further business in the everyday world, returned whence it came. No one has ever been able to give a fully satisfactory explanation of why ghosts can apparently make their presence known to some people but not to others in the same place and at the same time. The ghosts may not even be the returning spirits of humans. Ghostly phenomena associated with cats, dogs and horses, for example, have also been reported.

Children's fictional stories may have ghosts covered in white sheets, rattling chains and emitting screeching noises. In adult fiction the ghosts are generally more subdued or understated. In the works of that doyen of ghost story writers, M.R. James, the ghosts are little more than hints or suggestions. In spite of being so understated, they are capable of being extraordinarily menacing and malevolent. Truly the icy finger tracing out the spine.

Ghostly phenomena continue to exert a perennial interest even in a modern world dominated by the apparent rationalities of science and technology and a largely secular world deeply imbued with scepticism and cynicism. Each year priests carry out innumerable exorcisms in all seriousness intended to bring peace to the living and repose to the spirits of the dead.

Something atavistic, a vestigial sixth sense, can cause the hair to rise on the back of the neck at certain times and in certain places. Frissons of unease developing into fear may cause a rash of goose pimples for reasons we simply cannot explain. While we do not really like being spooked in real life, we love scary stories and most of us enjoy being comfortably scared. Ghosts are big business. Fictional ghost stories, ghost walks, films and documentaries about the paranormal have never been more popular. Spiritualism and psychic research are going strong and still trying to obtain the incontrovertible evidence that will sink the sceptics once and for all. Ghosts remain as much a part of popular culture as they were in the Middle Ages.

Do ghosts exist? If so, what are they? Do they have any objective existence or are they simply the product of superstitious minds, personal suggestibility or overheated imaginations? If we accept the claims of serious people that they have had experiences of a paranormal kind, what was it that they actually saw, heard or otherwise sensed? Isn't there a commonsense or perfectly mundane explanation for most or all of these phenomena? Even if we do not wish to probe too deeply into these questions, most of us can still appreciate a spooky story or movie or can keenly anticipate jumping out of our skins at the appropriate moment on a ghost walk. They are part of the rich and fascinating tapestry of fact, folklore, myth and legend. There are even serious academic studies written on the subject, such as the very readable *The Haunted: A Social History of Ghosts*, by Owen Davies, published in 2007.

One theory of haunting is that ghostly phenomena are a kind of spiritual film, a force generated in places where deeds of violence or great emotional upheavals have taken place. An energy is released which replicates at least some of the sights and sounds of these powerful events. This energy then allows the re-enactment of these events to be experienced from time to time by the still-living, or at least by those apparently receptive to paranormal or psychic phenomena. If there is any substance to this theory, it does account for the disappearance of some habitual or long-established haunting phenomena. The highly charged emotional ether simply dissipates over time.

If you ask people what kinds of places they expect to be haunted, they would probably include 'Gothic' semi-derelict mansions; the crypts used as charnel houses or bone-holes in some ancient churches; churchyards; hoary ivy-clad old ruins; dark and dingy castle dungeons; crossroads where gibbets used to display the mortal remains of executed highwaymen; and also the local 'lover's leap', the scene of years of tragic suicides provoked by the miseries of unrequited love. To some extent such scenes are clichés. The spiritual film idea, if it has any plausibility, helps to explain why the locations where ghostly activity is reported are often much more mundane. While railway locations such as tunnels, the overgrown formation of long-abandoned lines and closed stations in particular do seem to provide ideal scenarios for paranormal comings and goings, reports often come from everyday places such as level crossings, signal boxes, station footbridges and even the interior of well-occupied railway carriages.

We believe that some honestly presented reports of strange phenomena have unknown but entirely simple and everyday explanations. People subjected to experiences involving extreme emotions such as terror may not be reliable witnesses. Some reports are made by people seeking attention and publicity – a few days of capricious celebrity. Other reports are the work of deliberate hoaxes or sometimes of people who have allowed their imaginations to run away with them. With the stories mentioned in this book, we believe that the people involved genuinely experienced or sensed something odd. What that might be is not easily explained, and, of course, may not have been anything to do with the paranormal. We want to let the stories do the talking and we try to provide some historical background and railway detail as appropriate.

The railways of Britain cannot be seen in isolation. They were both a product of and a major contributor to the complex set of interacting economic and social developments which historians conveniently call the Industrial Revolution. This was the starting point of the modern world. The railways, in conjunction with the electric telegraph which was developed as an aid to safety, initiated the revolution in high-speed communication and transmission of information which continues to this very day. Of the early railways, the most significant was almost certainly the Liverpool & Manchester, opened in 1830. This joined two of the north's most important cities, was designed to use steam locomotives from the start and was soon bringing real economic benefits to the industrialists of south Lancashire

A tunnel ghost? Or a little photographic sleight of hand?

and Merseyside. It also had one almost totally unexpected effect – it showed that there was a market for people to travel just for the sheer pleasure of travelling.

Right from their inception, the railways elicited mixed responses from the public. Some regarded the steam locomotive as a frightening fiery devil, it and the iron road it ran on being unwelcome intruders into the placid English countryside, while others were fearful of its speed, of its lofty viaducts and especially its baleful tunnels. There were those, however, who found railways exciting for bringing places which had been distant closer together and for opening up opportunities for travel and adventure.

Any train, especially a steam train, takes on a more mysterious and romantic aura after dark, and many of the stories which follow are about experiences that occurred at night. Surprisingly, perhaps, there are relatively few good 'factual' railway ghost stories, given the social, cultural and wider impact of the railways. We have produced a selection of these, but omitted many where the phenomena described have been the same or very similar to the ones we have chosen, and we make no claim to providing a comprehensive guide to such tales or for an even geographical spread. Tunnels and signal boxes feature extensively, as do many level-crossings. Did the crossing-keeper go by the name of Charon?

We will leave this introduction with the words embossed on a cast-iron notice of the Great Northern Railway near Stafford, on its branch line from Derby and Uttoxeter. It was to be observed by engine drivers, and it read: 'Whistle at Cemetery Crossing'.

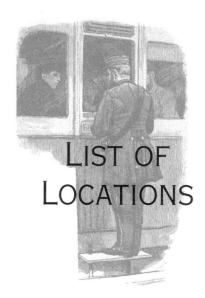

LIST OF LOCATIONS

THE STORIES

BUCKINGHAMSHIRE

High Wycombe

The first railway at High Wycombe was the Wycombe Railway, opened in 1854 from Maidenhead via Bourne End. It was leased to the Great Western Railway (GWR) and extended in 1862 through Princes Risborough to Thame, and later to Oxford. Subsequent lines gave High Wycombe direct services to Banbury, Leamington and Birmingham on the GWR, to Rugby and points north via Ashendon Junction and Brackley, by courtesy of the Great Central Railway, and to Paddington via Beaconsfield over the line of the Great Western & Great Central Joint. The line through High Wycombe is still operational

One night a railwayman had been having a drink or two with friends in a pub close to High Wycombe Station. Tearing himself away from the convivial company, he made for the station to catch a late train home to Beaconsfield. There were few people about at this time of the night, the station was quiet and the platform for his train was completely deserted when he got there. He had a few minutes to spare before the train was due. He then heard footsteps crunching along the ballast at track level. They approached and passed close by with no one visible to make the crunching! He heard the distinctive sound retreating into the distance, only to stop abruptly when some other passengers arrived on the platform. His train ran in and soon deposited him at Beaconsfield. He was not drunk nor was he given to flights of imagination but it was a puzzled and confused man who made his way home that night.

He often used High Wycombe Station and he knew several of the staff there. He hadn't been at all frightened by the strange invisible footsteps, but he couldn't get the experience out of his mind. He had little time for notions about ghosts and spooks and prided himself on being rational and level-headed. The next time he was there he mentioned what he had heard to one of the ticket collectors. This man didn't bat an eyelid. He and several other members of staff had heard the same disembodied footsteps. From time to time when the station was quiet, footsteps marched up to a particular door, and when the railway worker inside opened it, there was no one there. The men who had these experiences all thought a ghost was responsible but, oddly, none of them had ever felt frightened. After this, our man from Beaconsfield was never quite so adamant that ghosts were all products of the fevered imagination.

CAMBRIDGESHIRE

Conington

Conington is a small village, little more than a hamlet, and is close to the Great North Road about seven miles south of Peterborough. The very fine parish church of All Saints is some distance from the village and it possesses an especially magnificent west tower from about 1500 which can be seen, embowered in trees to the west, by travellers on the East Coast Main Line. Conington Crossing is something over a mile east of the church. It has the reputation of being haunted.

In March 1948 a light engine on the main line hit a lorry carrying German prisoners-of-war on this crossing. They were being taken to work on local fenland farms, and the accident which led to six of them dying happened at seven in the morning, on one of those days of dense fog that used to be so characteristic of this area. Later in 1948 an eminent citizen of Peterborough had been shooting in the fens with a companion, and he was killed instantly when his large and distinctive black Chrysler car was hit by an express train as it made its way over the crossing. On this occasion the visibility was excellent.

These two accidents followed any number of hair-raising narrow escapes over the previous decades, and a few fatalities. The road over the crossing was a very minor one which led to little more than a handful of farms, and traffic was very light. However, there was at that time no signal box to control the crossing and users had to open and close the gates as well as to get themselves across, exercising extreme vigilance because of the frequency and the speed of trains at this point. Unfortunately, users of the crossing were not always as careful as they needed to be and they sometimes took undue risks or forgot to close the gates after them. Footplate men on the locomotives that worked this stretch of line hated the place which had gained the reputation of being a serious danger spot. Pressure developed and eventually British Railways built a signal box to control the crossing.

Conington Crossing is remote, quiet and lonely. A shift at the new box, especially the shift between ten at night and six the next morning, was no sinecure. Trains were frequent, although people or vehicles wishing to cross the line were few. What made working the box such a challenge were the strange occurrences recorded by the signalmen. It didn't help that bitter winds howled across the fens, 'straight from Siberia', as they say in those parts, and they made the gates and other items of equipment rattle in a most disturbing way. Several signalmen reported the appearance of a large black limousine, clearly waiting to cross the line. When they went to open the gates, however, the car vanished. This weird and irritating event happened several times. The car did not restrict its appearance just to the hours of darkness; when it turned up during the day it still waited for the gates to be opened, but disappeared as soon as the signalmen went to do so. All were agreed that this was the black Chrysler which, with its occupant, had returned to the scene of the fatality. This spectral car was unnerving enough in its own right, but the local word was that the crossing was also haunted by the ghosts of the German prisoners-of-war. Some signalmen refused to work the box, especially on the night shift.

Conington Crossing is still there with or without its ghouls and spectres but the signal box was closed and demolished in conjunction with the establishment of a high-tech signalling centre at Peterborough in the 1970s. To this day, few people who know the area will volunteer to hang around at Conington Crossing, especially after dark.

Peterborough

In 1945 a married couple living in North London decided to visit relatives who lived in Newcastle-on-Tyne. The war was over and people just wanted things to get back to normal as quickly as possible. Many of the restrictions on travelling had been lifted, but the railway system was sorely run-down. Maintenance work had taken a back seat in the attempt simply to keep the vastly increased number of trains moving that were needed to support the war effort. Part of getting back to normal was to visit faraway relations, something that had been more-or-less impossible for the duration of the war.

The couple were not fond of train travel and so were looking forward somewhat glumly to the journey, expecting the train to be dirty, late and over-crowded. This had inevitably become almost the norm over the previous few years. They were therefore pleasantly surprised when they got to King's Cross not only to find their train with ease but to get seats in an otherwise unoc-cupied compartment. The train itself seemed reasonably clean, even to their somewhat jaundiced eyes. Not for them the pleasures of watching the moving scene as the train, headed by a Gresley A3 4-6-2, steamed northwards. They had bought a pile of newspapers at W.H. Smith to relieve the tedium of the journey.

Serried ranks of tall brickyard chimneys and a sulphurous smell indicated that the train was approaching Peterborough, its first booked stop. The train drew to a halt, there was some activity on the platform and passengers were walking up and down the side corridor. The compartment door slid open and an elderly lady entered carrying a sizeable wicker basket. She smiled at the couple and then sat down without saying a word. Her appearance had quite an effect on both husband and wife, although it was the wife who took in the details of the newcomer's appearance most keenly. The newcomer was dressed from head to toe in black. Her clothes were elegant and clearly of the highest quality. However, she was a walking anachronism! Every inch of her gave the impression of a prosperous Victorian lady of fashion. She looked very composed as she sat in the opposite corner, her face partly obscured by the brim of her sumptuous hat.

Grantham was the next stop and the train halted long enough for locomotives to be changed. The man decided he had time to get some tea from the refreshment room and he bought three cups – it was a kind thought that perhaps their new travelling companion might appreciate something to drink. He returned to the compartment and offered her one of the cups, which she took with a smile but, perhaps strangely, without saying anything.

Further calls were made at Doncaster, York and Darlington, but no one disturbed the silence in the compartment. Husband and wife continued to read the papers or to doze fitfully. The woman sat motionless, eyes closed. Every so often the man would peek at her. He didn't know exactly what, but there was definitely something odd about her – odd, that is, apart from the outdated fashion she sported. As the magnificent cathedral at Durham came into view, standing with the castle as its companion on the great rocky bluff above the River Wear, it was clear that this was where the woman was intending to leave the train. The man, ever gentlemanly, slid back the door for her and gestured that he would carry her basket. She smiled graciously, but without speaking, and stepped down onto the platform. The basket was strangely light, given its size. He handed it to her whereupon she spoke for the first time. 'I wish you many happy years,' she said. Having uttered these slightly enigmatic words, she vanished into thin air! Who was the lady in black who got on the train at Peterborough, sat in the compartment of the East Coast Main Line train and alighted at Durham that day in 1945?

Soham

On 2 June 1944, the 00.15 special freight train from Whitemoor to Earls Colne was travelling along the line from Ely to Fordham, approaching the small fenland town of Soham at around three in the morning. Driver Gimbert, aboard a W.D. 2-8-0, looked back and noticed that the wagon behind the tender was on fire. The train's payload consisted of bombs! Thinking quickly, but not panicking, Gimbert slowed the train and instructed fireman Nightfall to climb down and uncouple the wagon that was alight. This he did, and when he regained the footplate, locomotive and blazing wagon were moved forward.

Soham Station. This neat little station disappeared in the explosion.

The Soham signalman was standing on the platform and Gimbert told him that he intended to haul the wagon into a cutting just ahead where the force of any detonation, if one happened, would be at least slightly reduced. No sooner had he informed the signalman to this effect than an enormous explosion occurred. The wagon was reduced to matchwood, the locomotive severely damaged as it was blown off the rails, Fireman Nightfall was killed instantly, the signalman received injuries from which he died shortly afterwards and the 18-stone Gimbert was propelled through the air for a distance of 200 yards, sustaining serious but not life-threatening injuries.

There is no question that had Gimbert and Nightfall not taken the action they did, the entire train might have blown up and Soham would have been obliterated. As it was, almost every window in the town was broken and nearly every house received some damage. For their heroism Gimbert and Nightfall received well-deserved George Crosses, that for Nightfall unfortunately being posthumous. Their valour was recognised decades later when each of the men had a Class 47 diesel locomotive named after him.

It has been claimed that part of this drama is re-enacted in ghost form annually on the anniversary of the Soham Explosion. A steam locomotive hauling a freight train arrives at Soham from the Ely direction and is then detached. The apparition ends by simply fading away. Fortunately the explosion is not re-enacted. The line through Soham is still operational, although the station closed many years ago.

Yarwell Tunnel

The attractive stone-built village of Yarwell is in Northamptonshire, but Yarwell Railway Tunnel is in Cambridgeshire. The tunnel was on a long branch line to Peterborough from Blisworth, on what became known as the West Coast

Main Line. This cross-country route served Northampton, Wellingborough, Thrapston and Oundle. The line was built by the London & Birmingham Railway and opened to passenger traffic in June 1845 and goods traffic in December of that year. This was unusual. Usually lines opened for goods traffic before receiving official approval to run passenger trains.

The tunnel is over 600 yards long and provided a variety of problems during its construction. Conditions on the railway construction sites would have driven today's health and safety officials apoplectic. Deaths occurred among the navvies and labourers employed on the works. Some may have resulted from drunken brawls out of working hours. It was by no means unknown, however, for the navvies to work while inebriated. They did the hardest and most skilled work, and it was part of their laddish culture to take risks and cut corners. Doing so when drunk, of course, only made the dangers worse.

Whether it was the ghosts of the navvies making their presence felt we will never know, but men involved in maintenance work in the tunnel over the years told stories of the strange noises they heard. These included what sounded like fights, cries of pain, groans and various unidentifiable sounds. They made the tunnel an unpleasant place in which to be alone, although fortunately they usually did their work in small gangs. Also inexplicable was the disappearance of tools and pieces of equipment that would have been of little use to anyone else. A new piece of track laid on one particular day was found the following day having apparently been tampered with overnight. Many of the wooden keys strengthening the joint between the rails and the iron chairs spiked to the sleepers had been removed. This would have made the track unstable and could have led to an accident.

When work was being carried out on the track in the tunnel, it was customary to post lookouts at both entrances to give warning of an approaching train. On one occasion a gang was busy in the tunnel when a freight train rushed in, despite the fact that no warning had been given. Fortunately there were no injuries, but the men were somewhat shaken by the experience and they rather indignantly wanted to know why the lookout apparently hadn't been doing his job properly. They found him lying by the side of the track, uninjured but unconscious. When he came round he told the others that he had received a stunning blow on the head which knocked him out. This was puzzling because a doctor called to the scene could see no evidence of a blow. Equally puzzling was the fact that the lookout's equipment was also missing.

Wansford Station is not far from the eastern end of the tunnel. A past stationmaster used to carry out his duties almost always accompanied by his cat, Snowy. One early evening Snowy very unusually couldn't be found when it was time for his dinner. Having waited for an hour or so, the stationmaster decided to have a look at all the places where he knew that the cat liked to go. One of these was the tunnel, and the stationmaster entered, calling out Snowy's name. The man was near retirement and had become somewhat deaf,

Chester Station looking north. Nearby on the left stood a lead works. An employee there was killed on the railway and his ghost returned to stalk the works until they were demolished and houses built on the site.

and unfortunately he was struck down by a train and killed. Snowy never reappeared. Since the tragedy, a cat answering Snowy's description has been seen on occasions mewing pathetically at the entrance to the tunnel of ill-repute. Or is it the ghost of Snowy?

Passenger services through the tunnel on the Northampton to Peterborough route ceased on 2 May 1964 and those from Rugby to Peterborough finished in June 1966. Ironstone trains to Nassington ceased from December 1970 and vestigial freight services as far as Oundle on the Northampton line ended in 1972. However, all was not lost; the eastern end of the line from Peterborough eventually became the Nene Valley Railway, a heritage line unusual in that its loading gauge allows it to operate continental rolling stock. Trains began to run through the tunnel on a regular basis again in 1984.

CORNWALL

Bodmin Road
The landowners around Bodmin and the citizens of that town did not exactly welcome the proposal that their town should be an early addition

to the burgeoning railway network. The first schemes therefore came to naught, and it was not until 1874 that the Cornwall and West Cornwall railway companies proposed a branch from Bodmin Road on the main line from Plymouth to the west of Cornwall. When they discovered that the route proposed would require a lengthy and expensive tunnel they lost interest. However, when the London & South Western Railway Co. declared that it had Bodmin in its sights, the GWR – which had by now absorbed the two earlier companies – suddenly found that it cared so much for the welfare of Bodmin that it proposed to build a line to the town as soon as possible. It obtained parliamentary approval for the line from Bodmin Road on a different alignment from that originally suggested. The first sod was cut on 26 April 1884, and the line opened in 1887.

The Great Western's station at Bodmin was a fairly simple affair of the sort beloved by railway modellers. It and the rest of the branch led a quiet and unexceptional life, although an accident occurred close to Bodmin Road Station in 1903. A platelayer called Bricknell was in charge of two small trolleys loaded with old sleepers. They got out of control on a slight down gradient because a sudden heavy shower meant that the brakesticks he and his colleagues were using became completely ineffective. The trolleys collided and Bricknell was crushed to death. The coroner at the inquest made some acerbic comments about the GWR's safety arrangements, or, rather, the lack of them.

It was not long before the point at which the accident occurred gained the reputation of being haunted by a figure, described as being ghostly and ragged. It was both seen and heard by gangers walking the line during daylight hours and at dusk. It emitted ear-piercing screams of pain. Few who had this experience doubted that it was the ghost of the unfortunate Bricknell.

Bodmin Road in the GWR days. Note the curious arrangement to get water from the tank to supply locomotives at the platform-end.

St Keyne

The Liskeard & Caradon Railway opened in 1844 from Moorswater to South Caradon, a line designed to tap into the rich copper deposits and the resources of granite in the Caradon area of south Cornwall. At Moorswater the loads were transhipped into boats on the Liskeard & Looe Union Canal which conveyed the material to ships at the harbour at Looe. As the amount of minerals and stone being transported built up, the canal company decided that a railway line linked to the Liskeard & Caradon would save one lot of transhipment, and the resulting railway opened in 1860. In 1879 passengers began to be conveyed from Moorswater to Looe. In 1901 a steeply graded and sharply curved connection was put in which allowed trains from Looe to serve Liskeard Station on the Plymouth to Penzance main line.

The branch from Liskeard to Looe is miraculously still open for passengers, and on Mondays to Fridays enjoys a service of nine trains in each direction with one less on a Saturday. The line passes very near St Keyne's Well. This, in its delightful setting, is the source of several legends, but the main one, perhaps obviously, refers to St Keyne herself. She is supposed to have been one of twenty-six children fathered by the fifth-century Welsh King Brechan. Obviously a busy man, Brechan nevertheless must have found time to bring his offspring up well because no fewer than fifteen of them became saints, including, of course, Keverne herself. She was beautiful and a woman of the utmost probity who went round righting wrongs and performing miracles until the time came for her to retire. She chose a spot by the well and planted four trees there. a willow, an oak, an elm and an ash. Later, as she was dying, she blessed the well in verse as follows:

The quality that man or wife,
Whose chance or choice attains,
First of this sacred stream to drink,
Thereby the mastery gains.

Apparently the well became famous, at least in Cornwall, and many newly married couples would head for the well when the nuptials had ended, each hoping that by being the first to quaff a mouthful of its limpid waters, they would establish who wore the trousers in the marriage.

The poet Robert Southey (1774–1843) visited St Keyne's Well and felt impelled to mark the occasion and the legend in verse. Part of it goes like this, his poetic comment being that of someone worldly-wise:

I hasten'd as soon as the wedding was done,
And left my wife in the porch;
But I' faith she had been wiser than me,
For she took a bottle to church.

A neat but little-used halt. Its full name is St Keyne Wishing Well Halt, and it is a request stop on the Liskeard to Looe line. It all looks very tranquil by day, but ghost hunters have registered high levels of unexplained activity during the hours of darkness.

The custom certainly continued at least up to the twentieth century, and the story goes that one pair of newly-weds were on a Liskeard to Looe train heading to St Keyne. The young bride was so eager to get the upper-hand over the groom that she opened the carriage door before the train stopped, fell onto the line and broke her neck, dying instantly. This tragedy is thought by some to have imbued the halt and its surroundings with a mass of paranormal energy. Consequently, psychic investigators and ghost hunters have made many visits, usually at dead of night, and gathered much fascinating data. A young woman in a white bridal outfit is said to haunt the area around the well and the railway halt.

COUNTY DURHAM

Darlington, North Road Station
The Stockton & Darlington Railway was the first railway authorised by Parliament for the conveyance of goods and passenger traffic hauled by steam traction. This makes it of great historical importance despite the fact that few facilities were provided for passengers in its early years and that horses provided much of the traction. The line opened in 1825.

The S&D's first passenger station in Darlington was situated close to the present North Road Station which opened in 1842. Back in the 1850s this station witnessed a striking manifestation of the paranormal. A watchman used to patrol the station and its surroundings, which included the nearby goods depot. This particular night was a cold one and, having done a patrol, the man went to a room in the cellar of the station for a drink and some snap. No sooner was he sitting down than he was aware that he had company. Without having made any noise in entering, a stranger and a black retriever dog were eying him up. They were uninvited, they were trespassing and there was something odd, even eerie, about their appearance. Not bothering to ask questions, the watchman jumped up, hoping that by doing so he might persuade the unwelcome duo to leave. When they didn't he aimed a punch at the stranger. The watchman was a big and powerful man and the blow would have felled most mortals, but in this case it simply went through the figure in front of him and did so with such force that he injured his knuckles on the wall behind. By now he was aware that there was more to his visitors than met the eye, but his immediate thought that they were ghosts was modified somewhat when the stranger called out in pain and fell back as if the blow had landed on him fairly and squarely. As its master was going 'Ow!' the dog started to savage the watchman's leg. However, the visitors must have decided that enough was enough and they went through a door into the adjacent coal cellar. His blood boiling at this interruption of his routine, the watchman followed them into the coal cellar, but they had disappeared, despite the door being the only means of entrance or exit. Probing a heap of coal to see if his adversaries were hiding seemed pretty pointless and so the watchman returned to the cellar and his unfinished tea. The whole bizarre episode had taken less than a minute. His leg was throbbing with pain but it was strange that when he rolled his trousers up to examine the damage the dog had done with its fangs, there wasn't so much as a mark to be seen. What kind of a dog was it, he asked himself, which could cause such pain with no visible evidence?

The watchman, as the reader may have guessed, was no shrinking violet, and after work he was soon telling anyone who would listen about his nocturnal adventure. It was soon all over Darlington and, of course, there were some who thought he was just an attention-seeker. In the brouhaha brought about by his revelations, it was remembered that just a few years previously a railway clerk who was always accompanied at work by a black retriever had committed suicide in the same room where the watchman claimed to have encountered the apparitions. Some people accused him of having known this and used the information to get his moment in the limelight. Such taunts had no effect on the watchman, who never budged from his story.

Trains still call at North Road on their way to and from Darlington and Bishop Auckland. Most of what were the old station buildings are now occupied by the Darlington Railway Centre and Museum.

Darlington North Road. The train-shed in pre-grouping days.

CUMBRIA

Lindal Moor

Lindal was a wayside station on the main line of the small but enterprising Furness Railway from Carnforth to Barrow. This part of the line used to be in Lancashire. Large amounts of haematite iron ore were extracted in the district around Lindal, which consequently was riddled with underground workings. To service these workings, Lindal Ore Sidings were constructed, and it was at these sidings that one of railway history's most bizarre happenings occurred on 22 September 1892.

A Furness Railway goods engine, Class D1, No.115, nicknamed a 'Sharpie' after its builders, Messrs Sharp Stewart, was standing light engine in the sidings when suddenly there was an enormous rumbling sound and a huge crater opened up. The driver, Postlethwaite, and Fireman Robinson leapt for their lives as their 50-ton locomotive disappeared into the gaping hole. A breakdown gang was summoned from Barrow and they managed to extricate the tender. Removing the locomotive was going to be a more difficult matter and so they returned to Barrow for their heavy lifting gear. Imagine their surprise when, on their return, the locomotive was nowhere to be seen! It is thought to have ended up about 200ft down in the honeycomb of subterranean workings from which ore had been extracted and which had so unexpectedly collapsed.

It is still there, and local legend says that it is running on the Hades & District Underground Railway! Over the years there has been talk of recovering it. Now there's a challenge for railway preservationists! No.115 is effectively sealed in below ground and is quite probably largely unaffected by rust and corrosion, although it is likely to be bearing the scars from its fall.

Mining subsidence in the Lowfield Pit, which had workings beneath the railway, was blamed for this freakish occurrence and the Furness Railway Co., aware that other tracks in the area ran over similar subterranean workings, quickly had them packed with old railway sleepers in an attempt to prevent a similar incident in the future. It was not until the spring of 1893 that normal working was resumed at Lindal. Mining continued in the area and it was only half jokingly that the men used to quip about the new safety hazard, steam locomotives falling through the roof!

The line through Lindal opened in 1851 and the station closed in 1951, exactly a century later. The line remains operational but only a practised eye would be able to identify that at one time there were extensive sidings at this point. The route from Carnforth westwards along the northern side of Morecambe Bay and on viaducts across the estuaries of the Rivers Leven and Kent is a scenic delight even if the waters of Morecambe Bay have virtually ceased to lap the promenade at Grange-over-Sands.

Maryport

West Cumbria is a strange but fascinating part of the UK. It is out on a limb, not really being on the way to anywhere. People going to and from Scotland head up the West Coast Main Line or the M6, while others visiting the beauties of the Lake District do just that, and consider that Workington, Whitehaven and Maryport have little to offer. To travel by train from Lancaster via Barrow to Carlisle requires patience and fortitude. There are a few through trains. They take over three and a half hours – otherwise the passenger has to change at Barrow, taking even longer. This is a journey replete with visual interest but, especially when undertaken in one of those abominations known as a 'Pacer' diesel multiple-unit, it would only be a dyed-in-the-wool railway enthusiast who would consider doing it a second time.

West Cumbria has been and remains isolated, but it has a proud record of mining, industrial and maritime activity. Coal was extracted from outcropping seams near Whitehaven as early as the thirteenth century, but major exploitation of the district's coal and iron ore resources began in the eighteenth century and reached a peak in the following century. The area was exceptionally hard-hit in the years between the two world wars, and subsequently went into a recession from which it would not be unfair to say that it has never fully recovered. There is still much poverty in West Cumbria.

Few places in the area were harder hit than Maryport. In the inter-war years, unemployment in Maryport on occasions went as high as 80 per cent of the population of working age. In its heyday huge amounts of coal were exported through the docks, and many small ocean-going ships were built in the mouth of the River Ellen. Proposals to place the town on the expanding railway network were made as early as the 1830s. The first section of the Maryport & Carlisle Railway was opened in 1840 and completed throughout in 1845. Extensions were made under the auspices of other railway companies southwards down the coast through Workington, Whitehaven and Millom to Barrow.

In the 1930s a man, perhaps driven to distraction by Maryport's economic woes, threw his baby onto the railway line whereupon it was promptly run over by a train, receiving appalling injuries from which it died a few hours later. The man was hanged for the crime, but on occasions for many years after this needless tragedy the screams of a newborn baby in extreme agony resounded around the spot, much to the horror of local residents. The line through Maryport is still operational.

Tebay

The trains that rush up and down the West Coast Main Line today pass the small settlement of Tebay in the twinkle of an eye. To most travellers the name 'Tebay' only recalls a service area on the M6. To railway enthusiasts, however, the place has much greater significance. It stands at the bottom of the climb to Shap which, with Beattock Bank north of Lockerbie in Scotland, represented the most formidable inclines facing northbound Anglo-Scottish steam trains. The climb itself involves four miles on a gradient of 1 in 75. So formidable are the Cumbrian Fells that when a line from London, Crewe and Preston to Glasgow was first mooted, it was believed that the steam engines of the time would not be powerful enough to make the climb. Instead for a while passengers could travel to an obscure place on the Fylde Peninsula which came to be known as Fleetwood after a major local landowner. There they embarked on steamers for Ardrossan in Scotland. However, steam technology moved very quickly and locomotives became powerful enough to ascend these heights, albeit with a sturdy shove from behind with a banking engine.

The line over Shap was built by the Lancaster & Carlisle Railway and formally opened late in 1846. Tebay was the place chosen for an engine shed to house the bankers, and a settlement of houses and associated social facilities was built for the railway employees. In that sense Tebay was a railway village every bit as much as Crewe was a railway town. The sight of a steam locomotive at full stretch pounding up Shap with the banking engine blasting away with brute force at the back was an awesome one, and also highly photogenic. Tebay and the lonely country abutting the climb to Shap became the haunt of generations of railway enthusiasts and some very fine photographs by the likes of Ivo Peters, Eric Treacy and Derek Cross survive to give an idea of the heroic physical efforts required by the crews of heavy trains climbing the bank. Steam working over Shap continued almost to the bitter end of regular steam power in the UK, and in the last few years enthusiasts from far and wide made the pilgrimage to enjoy and record a scene they knew was about to disappear.

Engine sheds were potentially very dangerous places and official entry was prohibited to all except those with written permission. However, notices not to trespass in such places did little to deter most railway enthusiasts who exercised great ingenuity in finding ways to 'bunk' sheds, this being slang for getting round them without a permit. We do not know whether the enthusiast concerned had permission, but he visited Tebay shed in 1967 to photograph some of the last generation of banking engines. These were Standard Class '4' 4-6-0s, and a pretty rundown lot they were by this time. Tebay was only a small shed and just two locomotives were present when he visited. There didn't seem to be anyone about, even if he had tried to ask for permission. Apart from the sizzle and gurgle of these two engines in light steam, the place was as silent as a grave. Anyway, he took what photographs he could and left, still rather puzzled by the apparent total lack of living beings in the shed. Imagine his surprise when his photographs came back from the processor and there in several of the pictures was a human figure staring at the camera with a slightly enigmatic expression. Even more enigmatic was that the figure was diaphanous and details of the locomotive in front of which he was standing could clearly be seen. He knew the figure had not been there when he took the photographs. Was it a ghost?

DERBYSHIRE

Chesterfield

The main line of the former Midland Railway leaving Chesterfield in a northerly direction shares the valley of the River Rother with the A61 trunk road and the Chesterfield Canal. Just to the north of Chesterfield is Tapton Junction where a freight-only line diverges to the east and avoids Sheffield passing via Staveley on its way to Rotherham. The main line heads for Sheffield via Dronfield and Dore.

On the hillside east of the railway at Tapton Junction stands Tapton House, now part of Chesterfield College of Further Education, about a mile from the town centre. It was to Tapton House that George Stephenson (1781–1848), often called 'the Father of the Railways', retired to spend the last ten years of his life. He had been born in humble circumstances but his was a life of rich achievement and he became a wealthy man with a host of business interests in railways, coal mines and ironworks, for example. He had never lost his broad Geordie accent nor had he cultivated much in the way of refined manners but he was on intimate terms with many of the 'movers and shakers' of his generation and there were frequently distinguished guests at his house. They tended to be hard-headed practical people like himself. He had little time for the idle fops of the aristocracy and gentry.

He remained very active during his years at Tapton and took great pleasure in the grounds of the house and in gardening. One of his less well-known endeavours was an attempt to cultivate a perfectly straight cucumber. While this was a worthy task in itself, and one to which he brought all his customary resource and determination, it was fated to be unsuccessful.

The final resting place of George Stephenson's mortal remains is under the communion table in Trinity Church, close by. It seems, however, that his spirit could not abide to be away from his beloved Tapton House, and what is thought to be his ghost is seen from time to time moving from room to room as if in search of something. Not only seen but heard, because on occasions the ghost asks, ever so politely but in a Geordie accent you could cut with a knife, for a cup of tea.

The problem of the cucumber remains unresolved.

Left: George Stephenson. The 'Father of the Railways' became rich and famous but never lost his thick north-eastern accent.

Below: A view looking north from Chesterfield Station in the direction of Tapton.

Tunstead Farm

The line from Buxton northwards to Chapel-en-le-Frith, New Mills and Stockport was opened in 1863. It was initially operated by the Stockport, Disley & Whaley Bridge Railway and absorbed by the London & North Western Railway in 1866. The building of the line had not been easy. Any plan for public passenger-carrying railway lines had to be presented to Parliament in the form of a Bill to be considered by both Houses. If it was passed, it became what was known as a Local and Personal Act which, among other things, would equip the company concerned with rights for compulsory purchase. These would be exercised where landowners were unwilling to sell land or buildings, and one such place where this happened was Tunstead Farm. This remote place overlooked the railway between Chapel-en-le-Frith and Whaley Bridge, and it also overlooked Coomb Reservoir. The terrain is very hilly in this neighbourhood and the engineering works were correspondingly heavy. The route had been surveyed to cross part of the land associated with Tunstead Farm but so many problems were encountered with the embankments on this section of line and with bridges that collapsed and had to be rebuilt that eventually the company decided on a new route avoiding Tunstead Farm altogether. The engineers encountered far fewer problems on this adjacent new alignment and the work went ahead quickly. The company let it be known that geological conditions had forced the change of route. Local people knew otherwise.

Dickie o' Tunstead is the name given to an ancient human skull which is kept at Tunstead Farm. Local legend says that it is the skull of one Ned Dixon, who was murdered by his cousin in the farmhouse. Any attempt to disturb it or particularly to move it out of the house will set in motion a series of accidents and even disasters which will only stop when the skull is restored or apparently reassured that no further disruption will take place. Nodding their heads sagely, the local wiseacres knew why the path of the line was altered. Dickie o' Tunstead had made sure that it would.

Legends of skulls that take umbrage when the even tenor of their lives is disrupted can also be found at Burton Agnes Hall in East Yorkshire and Bettiscombe Manor in Dorset.

DORSET

Bincombe Tunnel

Weymouth was for a while almost the prototype of the fashionable as opposed to the popular English seaside resort. The town, which before the eighteenth century had largely been thought of as a decayed seaport, hit the headlines when in 1789 George III, no less, arrived, accompanied by the usual flock of medical advisers, bumptious officials and busybodies, court-followers, lounge lizards and toadies. The King was not a well man and he was in Weymouth to take advantage of the newly discovered therapeutic effects of sea–water. More specifically, he was there to bathe in the said water. After a few days breathing in the fresh sea air and viewing the sights, he allowed himself to be placed in a bathing machine and drawn out a short distance into the sea. He had squeezed himself into a costume which did little to hide the royal humps and bumps, and no sooner had he partially emerged to test the temperature of the water with his big toe than a band craftily hidden away in a nearby bathing machine struck up *God save the King*. They could scarcely have rendered the King's first dip in the briny more public had they executed a 24-gun salute.

These stirring events took place in 1789 and the King returned regularly to Weymouth until 1805, thereby guaranteeing the town pole position in the list of places that a certain class of person went in order to see and be seen. In the years that followed, however, other seaside resorts were busy copying Weymouth's example. The railways played an important role in bringing the visitors on whom these places depended, and many of these resorts were much handier for London than far-distant Weymouth. By the 1840s Weymouth was well and truly in the doldrums and needed urgently to be connected to the country's developing railway system. Southampton was joined to Dorchester naturally enough by the Southampton & Dorchester Railway in 1847. It was not until 1857, however, that its trains (having been taken over by the London & South Western Railway) could reach Weymouth by virtue of running powers over a line of the Great Western from Bristol, Bath, Frome and Yeovil.

A local for Weymouth drifts out of the southern entrance to Bincombe Tunnel, the next stop being the quaintly named Upwey Wishing Well Halt. The locomotive is a 45XX 2-6-2T.

The GWR had reluctantly agreed to install mixed-gauge track, and the GWR and LSWR started their services to Weymouth on the same day. This at long last gave the town access to London, strangely enough right from the start, by means of two different routes.

Bincombe Tunnel stands on the section of line between Dorchester and Weymouth where it passes on a steep gradient under Ridgeway Hill. Its involvement in the world of the possibly supernatural was short-lived. In 1991 several train drivers reported that while passing through the tunnel they had hit what was described as a 'substantial object'. This experience was made all the more unnerving because they thought it was a human body, either of someone who had been unaware of the approaching train or a person bent on committing suicide. This of course would be a traumatic experience for the unfortunate drivers. British Transport Police investigated each report but found absolutely nothing that could explain what the drivers had seen. As abruptly as the sensations in Bincombe Tunnel started, so they finished.

The line through Bincombe Tunnel is still operational.

GLOUCESTERSHIRE

Charfield

Charfield was a wayside station on the Birmingham to Bristol main line of the former Midland Railway, situated to the north-east of Bristol. Early on the morning of 13 October 1928 a Wolverhampton to Bristol goods train was being shunted back off the main line to clear the way for a fast overnight mail train from Leeds to Bristol. This train overran signals and crashed into the reversing goods train, part of which was still fouling the main line. A freight train from the Bristol direction was slowly passing at the time, and the mail train locomotive, coming off the rails, crashed into it. Three trains were therefore involved. Exactly at the point of impact there was a low over-bridge, and the carriages of the mail train piled up under this bridge and immediately caught fire. If anything can be said to be fortunate about the accident it was that the mail train was carrying few passengers. Fifteen died. The fire raged for twelve hours.

Among the dead were two children, a boy of about eleven and a girl perhaps two, maybe three, years younger. Although they were travelling together it seems that there was no adult accompanying them. This itself was rather odd because they were young to be travelling unaccompanied and especially at night. They had been observed by the fireman of the mail train chatting to the guard at Birmingham New Street. The fireman said that both children were well dressed and that the boy was wearing a school uniform. The guard was unable to add anything to this rather incomplete description of the children. He had died in the fire. Those bodies recovered from the mail train were so badly burned that there was no chance of them being identified. They were buried in the local parish churchyard and the LMSR, successor to the Midland Railway, erected a memorial with the names of those buried close by. They obviously could not name the boy and girl. They are remembered on the memorial as 'Two Unknown'.

Three mysteries are associated with the tragedy of these two children. The first is that the LMSR initially denied that the children had been on the train and argued that they must have been trespassing on the line at Charfield and were caught up in the accident, simply a case of being in the wrong place at the wrong time. The fireman of the mail train refuted this, stating that he saw them board the train at New Street. Why should the LMSR have lied?

Secondly there were some people who did not believe that the children or perhaps some of the other passengers were buried at Charfield at all but that their remains were spirited away by a military ambulance that was unaccountably present at the scene after the accident. No records exist as to why this vehicle was there. Thirdly, the death of two small children was obviously a tragedy. Why is it that no one ever came forward to say that they were the parents or guardians? Somebody presumably paid their fare at New Street and saw that they joined the right train. Someone else must have had the job of meeting them at their destination. They never came forward either. It was as if the children had never existed.

Some people claim that every year on the anniversary of the Charfield accident a woman in black is seen by the memorial in the churchyard. She looks

Memorial in the churchyard to the victims of the Charfield accident.

grief-stricken and is generally reckoned to be the mother of the two unfortunate children.

The route between Birmingham and Bristol was an amalgam of different schemes and was open throughout in the early 1840s. Charfield closed for passengers along with other small intermediate stations on the line in 1965, but the line is still operational.

GREATER LONDON

Addiscombe

Addiscombe was the terminus of a service via London Bridge and New Cross from Cannon Street Station in the city. The line to Addiscombe itself was built by the South Eastern Railway and opened in 1864. Although, of course, the service was initially operated with steam trains, it became part of the Southern Railway's expansive suburban network in the 1920s and a depot for electric multiple units was built where the old shed for steam locomotives used to be.

The depot for the electrics quickly gained a reputation for being haunted. A catalogue of phenomena was recorded. The old electric carriages were of course of the 'slam-door' variety. It was the job of the staff at Addiscombe Station to ensure that all the passengers had got off the last trains of the night before they went to the depot for cleaning and maintenance. The electric units should therefore have been empty except for their crews when they snaked their way into the depot. Some nights were punctuated by the sound of compartment doors slamming as if dozens of passenger had woken up from their snoozes, panicked when they realised where they were and leapt out of the trains, slamming the doors behind them in their urgency to get away. The sound of invisibly slamming doors being slammed by equally invisible belated travellers had an understandably disturbing effect on the night-shift staff.

When the trains came into the depot, the shoes picking up the current from the electric third rail would be isolated and, as a further precaution, the hand-brakes were screwed down. However, on many occasions members of staff relaxing over a mug of tea in the rest room would hear the sound of moving trains only to go outside and, as they expected, see that everything was just as it should be. The brake compressors which were isolated with all the rest of the electrical equipment would sometimes start making their rhythmic throbbing noise during the night even though no member of staff had been in the cabs of any of the units.

A mysterious figure was often seen in the environs of the depot sometimes apparently supervising the shunting of the units into the right positions for their departure in the morning. On occasions the same or another figure would be seen approaching a member of staff. This apparition had a menacing bearing but it used to vanish before any member of staff could recognise its facial features. Was this the force that also sometimes invisibly opened and closed the tight-fitting door to the rest room?

The depot had been the scene of a number of accidents leading to fatalities, and those who worked there reckoned that the ghost or ghosts were the spirits of these men whose lives were so tragically cut short.

The old Addiscombe Station and the depot itself no longer exist. They were closed when the Croydon Tramlink opened in 2000. The tram station currently called Addiscombe is on a different site. What happened to the ghosts?

GREATER MANCHESTER

Ashton Moss

There were three signal boxes at Ashton Moss. They were, respectively, Ashton Moss North Junction, Ashton Moss South Junction and OA&GB Junction. These initials stood for Oldham, Ashton & Guide Bridge Junction Railway, a line authorised in 1857 to join the oddly named station at Oldham Mumps to Ashton-under-Lyne and Guide Bridge. The railway network in this part of the eastern environs of Manchester was extremely complicated, the result of the wheeling and dealing, back-stabbing, outwitting and swindling which marked the activities of rival railway companies fighting for access to potentially lucrative traffic. This area associated especially with the cotton industry and coal-mining seemed extremely promising. This manner of conducting business helps to explain the almost labyrinthine welter of lines that could once be found in many of Britain's former manufacturing and mining areas.

One day in early 1975, the signalman at OA&GB Junction was a little surprised to hear footsteps climbing the external wooden staircase to his box. Visits from other railway workers were by no means uncommon, platelayers and suchlike dropping in for a cup of tea, a smoke and a chinwag, but this was Saturday afternoon and these men would mostly be enjoying time away from work, perhaps at a football match. The signalman saw the figure of a man he did not think he recognised reaching the top of the stairway. The doors of signal boxes rightly had a notice stating 'no admission'. Concentration was a vital part of a signalman's duty and management frowned on the idea of other railway workers using signal boxes for social purposes. Their presence, even unintentionally, might distract the attention of the 'bobby', as signalmen were called. They were rightly even more disapproving of members of the public visiting signal boxes without official permission. Working in a signal box could be lonely and on those occasions when there was little traffic around, it could most certainly be boring. No wonder that those signalmen who were of gregarious nature often welcomed a visit – even if it was from someone they didn't know who wanted to get an idea of how signalmen conducted their business.

The signalman waited for a knock, and when that didn't happen he walked across to the door and flung it open. There was no one there! The footsteps had been clearly audible coming up the steps; how could anyone have gone back down them in complete silence? Puzzled, the signalman descended and had a look around. He couldn't go far in case his bells sounded and required a response, but as he climbed back up to his eyrie he was deeply perplexed. He had found nothing to suggest that there had been anyone in the vicinity, and yet he was convinced the footsteps had been real.

The next Saturday he was working the same shift when, just as dusk was falling, he heard a noise down at track level in front of the box. He slid back the windows and thought he saw someone down on the track some distance away. He got on the circuit phone to his colleague at the neighbouring Ashton Moss Junction who said that he could also see what he thought was someone on the line. They both informed control and decided to leave their respective boxes and see if they could apprehend the person – a foolhardy trespasser perhaps, or maybe someone looking to steal line-side equipment. They found nothing.

They were two sober, steady and conscientious men. They were convinced that someone had been down on the line, someone who apparently had the ability to disappear at will. Neither of the men had any time for the supernatural. We have to ask whether the figure was the ghost of a railwayman or someone else who had perhaps been killed on that stretch of line in some long-forgotten incident. The men never experienced the same phenomenon again.

The only line past the former Ashton OA&GB Junction which is still operational is that from Manchester to Stalybridge, Huddersfield and Leeds. It carries passenger trains on a frequency that could not have been conceived of back in the 1970s.

The uninspired access to
Ashton-under-Lyne Station in
the Greater Manchester suburbs.

Bradley Fold

Bradley Fold was an intermediate station on what became a through line owned by the Lancashire & Yorkshire Railway Co. This was an important route enabling trains from Merseyside to bypass Manchester from the north on their way to the West Riding of Yorkshire, and vice versa. The line also provided connections between a string of important intermediate towns such as Wigan, Bolton, Bury and Rochdale. The line through Bradley Fold opened to passenger and freight traffic in December 1848.

Bradley Fold was three miles west of Bury and had the semi-industrial, semi-rural atmosphere common to much of this part of what was then Lancashire. A small community was gathered around a nearby cotton mill. The station possessed a level crossing. It enjoyed a reasonably generous service of local stopping trains in addition to a few passing expresses and many heavily laden freight and mineral trains. The flow of these latter trains meant that the signal box was manned continuously for twenty-four hours each weekday. Duty on the night shift, ten in the evening to six the following morning, meant a lonely vigil, and was definitely not for those who were blessed with too much imagination.

To carry out the duties of a signalman effectively, concentration, alertness, scrupulous attention to the rules, a tidy mind and a systematic approach were absolute necessities. These qualities were displayed in plenty by a man who joined the railway in the 1950s after service in the Royal Navy. After training, he enjoyed his work, although he realised that it involved a very considerable burden of responsibility. One momentary lapse of concentration could lead to an appalling catastrophe. The man was naturally conscientious and made a good impression on the equally conscientious man alongside of whom he worked while he was undergoing training. The two of them recognised kindred spirits and became firm friends.

The two men were frequently on alternate shifts and would often share a short overlapping period at the end and the beginning of their respective shifts when they would have a chat over a steaming mug of tea. Our ex-Navy man had taken to his duties as if tailor-made for them, but it wasn't long before he began to notice a degree of unease in his friend's demeanour. This culminated in his friend telling him that he could stand it no longer and was leaving the job at the first available opportunity. Concerned but unwilling to intrude on his friend's private thoughts, he wondered whether his friend had had any brushes with authority or any unpleasant experiences while at work. It was not unknown for vandals to find the windows of lonely signal boxes a tempting target even when they were manned. There was also coal and various copper and electrical fittings which provided temptation to the light-fingered fraternity. A signalman in such a lonely box could easily feel vulnerable.

He was on duty one night and dealing with a succession of trains in the witching hours. All traffic movements had to be recorded in the signal box's train register, and he was just about to make some entries when he heard the unmistakeable sound of footsteps crunching the ballast close to his box. He grabbed a torch, opened the door, descended to rail level and flashed the light hither and thither, but to no effect. There was no one there.

Even a fairly stolid man would have been disconcerted to hear disembodied footfalls so close by, and he spent the rest of the shift trying unsuccessfully to make some sense of what he had heard. He returned to the box for his turn of duty the next night wondering whether his imagination had been playing tricks. At the same time in the early hours of the next morning he again heard the footsteps. By now he was aroused and determined to make sure that anybody out there playing at silly buggers wouldn't do it again in a hurry. He grabbed a heavy poker and his torch and rushed down the steps. Again, nothing. Feeling indignation more than fear, he climbed back into the box and settled down, there being a gap in the procession of passing trains. Within a few minutes he heard a strange whistling noise apparently coming from outside the back of the box. Once more he took up poker and torch and descended to the track, absolutely sure that someone was taking liberties. He searched the area thoroughly but again found nothing.

Nothing untoward happened for an hour, when he decided to get some fresh air. He opened the door and stood at the top of the steps. It was a beautiful still night, only the bark of a fox or an occasional distant motorbike disturbing the otherwise almost tangible and immense silence around him. Suddenly he felt a wave of fear flooding over him and became convinced that his every move was being watched by eyes all the more threatening because he had no idea where they were. As he stepped back into the box, had he caught sight of some kind of fleeting shadow up near the ceiling? He could not be sure, but he felt certain that he was not alone and that something invisible was scrutinising his every move. How pleased he was when his shift ended.

On the third night and at the same time he heard the footsteps once more. He was clearly a man of courage because although his nerves were by now becoming somewhat shredded, he once again took up his poker and torch and rushed down the stairs. The sound of footsteps faded away to be followed to his horror by an ear-piercing scream close by. He flashed his torch in the direction of the sound and saw to his horror what looked like a human body lying by the side of the track. As he went to investigate, wondering whether someone had been knocked down by a train, the thing on the ground simply faded away.

He had now decided that he too would now look for another job on the railway which did not involve night shifts in lonely signal boxes at spots where such unnerving things happened. He lost touch with his friend, but some years later he discovered that a man had been killed on the line close to his box. He also learned that other signalmen had had similar experiences on the night shift but understandably had chosen to keep their experiences to themselves for fear that their colleagues might ridicule them or that

Bradley Fold Station Signal box. A typical timber-built Lancashire & Yorkshire Railway Co. wayside signal box.

management might think they were not up to the job. Had his friend also had similar experiences?

The line through Bradley Fold lost its passenger services in 1970. Freight services followed shortly after.

Manchester Mayfield

This was Manchester's 'forgotten' railway terminus. By the first decade of the twentieth century the six platforms of the London & North Western Railway Co.'s part of London Road Station were proving inadequate for handling the growing traffic, particularly the increase in the number of suburban trains when the Styal Line opened. The London Road site could not be expanded and so a decision was taken to build an 'overspill' station as close by as possible. This station, known as Manchester Mayfield, was opened in 1910. It was small, having only four platforms, and was joined to its 'parent', London Road, by a long and gloomy enclosed footbridge.

It was used on a regular basis by various short-haul suburban services and regular travellers may have resented the walk to get to Mayfield, but at least they knew the ropes. The station was also used as an 'overspill' for long-distance trains at particularly busy periods such as summer Saturdays. Many were the stories of woebegone passengers arriving with very little time to spare at London Road only to find to their bemusement or fury that their train was scheduled to leave immediately from the Mayfield platforms, which were best part of half a mile away! Then followed a heart-palpitating dash with their luggage along London Road's platforms, up the steps, along the footbridge and down into Mayfield, with the odds being that the traveller would be just in time to see his train steaming away into the distance.

Occasional travellers may not even have been aware that Mayfield existed and, indeed, it spent its life thoroughly in the shadow of its mighty neighbour. A massive rebuilding of London Road Station took place in association with the electrification of the lines to Crewe and later Stoke, Stafford and London Euston. This eliminated the need for Mayfield's extra capacity and it closed to passengers on 26 August 1960. The rebuilt London Road Station opened on 12 September 1960 and was renamed 'Manchester Piccadilly', although 'London Road' did actually give a much better idea of exactly where the station was located in the city.

Mayfield was never a very prepossessing station, and it did not help that it was hit by a German bomb during the Second World War. Those who worked there may either have welcomed it as a rest cure after the hurly-burly of London Road or Manchester's other three big stations or resented the feeling that they had been shunted into a semi-forgotten backwater. Whether this was responsible we will never know, but one station worker hanged himself in a cabin full of electrical equipment, and a foreman allowed things to get so much on top of him that he also hanged himself, but did so in the gentlemen's toilets. A porter on the night shift fell to his death down the shaft of the luggage lift.

These events may have hung like a pall over the place, and Mayfield got a reputation for being spooked. Footsteps were heard walking deserted platforms on many occasions in the hours of darkness. One rail worker on the night-shift was sitting in his cabin when slouching footsteps shuffled past. He opened the door to peek out. No one was there but a distinct chill could be felt on what was actually a very humid summer's night. One man twice experienced footsteps dogging his own as he walked to the station entrance in the middle of the night, having just finished his shift. Although scared, on the second occasion he was near the main collection of switches for the station lights and he flicked on all those which had been turned off in the semi-darkened station. Nothing was there.

In 1970 Mayfield became a rail-served parcels depot, and continued in that role until 1986 since when it has been disused, although it provided an ideal base for a drug dealer's activities in an episode of the excellent TV drama *Prime Suspect*. At the time of writing (autumn 2008) the shell of Mayfield is still there. Various proposals have been made for it to return to use as a passenger station, to become a coach station or be part of a comprehensive

Typical LNWR lower-quadrant signals guard the approach to and exit from Manchester Mayfield Station.

redevelopment of this underused quarter on the fringe of the city centre. The ghosts, meanwhile, can roam in peace.

HAMPSHIRE

Hayling Island
Hayling Island is a low-lying island standing between Chichester Harbour in the east and Langstone Harbour in the west. It enjoyed quite a vogue as a minor resort before British holidaymakers took advantage of cheap air travel to those foreign parts where sunshine is more surely guaranteed. Sailing is possible, as is windsurfing, and some people regard Hayling Island as the place where the latter sport was invented. The island is joined to the mainland at Havant by a road bridge.

The Hayling Railway Co. opened a line across a timber viaduct from Havant in 1867 and the London, Brighton & South Coast Railway took over in 1872. The Langstone Viaduct was of comparatively light construction which placed severe restrictions on the locomotives that could work over it. The LBSCR's tiny but powerful 'Terrier' tank engines proved absolutely ideal and came to monopolise the working, and will for ever be associated with the quaint little branch line. The line generated great affection and was known as 'Hayling Billy'. Unfortunately it did not generate similarly great revenue.

The line closed in 1963 but for some years after there were reports that the neighbourhood of the old Hayling Island Station was haunted by the ghost of a railway guard who had worked on the line back in the 1930s and '40s and presumably couldn't bear to be parted from it even in death. Other people claimed that the ghost was none other than that of a former stationmaster at Hayling Island.

Swanwick

Swanwick is a station on the Fareham to Netley and Southampton line which is still operational. The section through Swanwick was opened in 1889 by the London & South Western Railway.

In 1971 a man standing on Swanwick Station late one night was watching his only fellow-passenger. It was a woman who looked distressed and confused. She was crying and kept repeating the words, 'I can't go back.' The train arrived and he wanted to help her get on because it was the last train that night. However, the guard was getting impatient with both of them and so he had no option but to leave her behind. Her evident distress worried him and he decided to phone the police when he got off the train. He did this, telling them where she was and that he thought she was probably at risk – perhaps suicidal. Next day he was browsing through a local paper which contained a story about a woman who had been hit and killed by a train at Swanwick a couple of nights earlier. There was a photograph of the victim. It was the distressed woman he had seen only the night before.

View of the Swanwick Station buildings from the street. The station is served by trains running between Southampton and Portsmouth.

HERTFORDSHIRE

Hatfield

After legal and parliamentary wrangling of monumental proportions, in 1846 the Great Northern Railway obtained sanction to build a main line from London to the neighbourhood of Doncaster. Services began in 1850. Some were long-distance expresses, but shorter-distance trains which we would now probably call outer-suburban ran from London to Hatfield to a station which was on a slightly different site from the current one.

The paranormal experience at Hatfield definitely casts the ghost in a positive role as a benefactor. In the 1900s a non-stop passenger train was passing through the platforms at the old Hatfield Station. The driver was rather put out when what he described as 'an insubstantial man' apparently leapt onto the footplate despite the fact that the train was moving quite quickly. This apparition, who exuded an unpleasant chilliness, somehow made it clear to the driver that he must slow the train and stop at the next station going southwards, which was Potters Bar. On arrival there the driver, already shaking like a leaf, started shaking more violently, but with relief rather than fear because he saw ahead of his train a large obstacle on the line. If he had continued at his normal speed the train would have crashed into this obstacle and there might have been a frightful accident. Turning round to express his gratitude, he realised that the apparition had vanished. What is to be made of this?

ISLE OF WIGHT

Newport

The Isle of Wight has often been described as a microcosm of southern England, although it is only twenty miles east and west by thirteen miles north and south. Its entire route mileage was a mere forty-five miles, and yet the lines involved had originally been projected by no fewer than six separate companies. The first line to be opened on the island was the Cowes & Newport in 1862. If anywhere was the hub of the railways on the Isle then it would have to be Newport. From there lines radiated north, south, east and west.

Since the lines closed, there have been many reports of strange phenomena around the site of the former railway installations at Newport. At the site of the old station, a man looking like a platelayer has been seen walking along swinging a lantern, and he has the ability to walk through walls and doors. A steam train with three coaches has been reported travelling soundlessly along the formation of one of the old lines. Others claim to have heard this ghost train. Yet other people claim to have seen *and* heard it.

Newport can be described as the hub of the Isle of Wight's former extensive railway system.

KENT

Pluckley

The strategic importance of Dover as the gateway to and exit from England inevitably meant that the building of a line between it and London was discussed at an early stage. The first company to build such a line would be able to tap into a major and lucrative source of traffic. The South Eastern Railway grabbed the opportunity, and its main line was authorised by Parliament in June 1836. The line was opened in sections and completed throughout to Dover in 1843. Pluckley is the last station before Ashford on the line from London.

Pluckley has the reputation of being England's most haunted village. The ghosts come in various forms and several are associated with the local landowning family, the Derings. A 'Red Lady' wearing a fifteenth-century gown flits around the church and the churchyard, apparently searching for the burial place of her baby. The family lived in a manor house nearby which burnt down, but the site is haunted by a 'White Lady' holding a red rose who occasionally also puts in an appearance in the churchyard. Mysterious noises have been heard issuing from the Dering chapel in the church. There is a pub with a poltergeist, a ghostly monk, a ghostly miller and a spectral tramp (piquant variations on normal themes), a spooky old gypsy woman and the ghost of a highwayman who, as his kind tend to do, lurks by a crossroads which in this case has the lovely name of Fright Corner. Others could be mentioned. Just for good measure, the railways have got in on the act. The ghost of a man knocked down and killed by a train has been seen on the track near the station,

A weather-boarded station building, very appropriate to Kent. This all looks very peaceful given that some people say that Pluckley is the most haunted village in England.

and steam trains have been heard whistling on many occasions since regular steam operations ceased. No one claims to have seen the locomotive doing the whistling.

LANCASHIRE

Bispham

Blackpool and trams are as inseparable as fish and chips. Trams started operating in Blackpool in 1885 along part of the seafront, and this line was actually the first electric street tramway in Britain. By 1892 these trams were operating between the North and South Pier.

In 1898 a more ambitious operation was started by the Blackpool & Fleetwood Electric Tramway Co. which linked Blackpool North Station with Fleetwood via a line which mostly ran close to the coast and which included stretches of reserved track. In 1920 Blackpool Corporation bought the company and combined its operations with their own.

Trams started becoming unfashionable in the UK in the 1930s, being thought of as outdated and too redolent of the working class and of Victorian England. Much of Blackpool's tram system was replaced by motor buses and the only route to survive has been that on the continuously built-up part of The Fylde between Starr Gate and Fleetwood. It is now operated by Blackpool Transport Services Limited.

A few miles north of central Blackpool is the suburb of Bispham. Here at the northern extremity of the resort's famous 'illuminations' is one of the most grandiose tram stops anywhere in the world. Vastly outdoing many of today's minimalist unmanned railway halts, this building draws attention to itself by the words 'Bispham Station' incised above what can only be described as a portico. It was built in 1932. After having waxed so enthusiastic about this tram station, the authors have to accept that its connection with the world of ghosts is something of an anti-climax. On stormy nights a figure has been seen close to the station, walking purposefully along the track and carrying a lamp. As with so many of its kind, this mysterious figure vanishes when approached. No one seems to have any idea who he is and why he chooses to walk only in bad weather.

Entwistle

The line through Entwistle opened in 1848. It joined the important industrial towns of Bolton and Blackburn and came under the control of the Lancashire & Yorkshire Railway. This line passes through surprisingly green countryside giving the lie to the idea that south Lancashire was all satanic mills and chimneys. The station, which is located on a long climb from Bolton at 1 in 74, stood about 690ft above sea level and is a bleak spot for much of the time. It was an odd station with an island platform and an elevated signal box on girders straddling the tracks bypassing the platform. The line, now reduced to two tracks, is still operational although reduced in importance and carrying much less traffic.

In the late 1930s there were several occasions when the ethereal-looking figure of a child was seen running across the tracks and then, still running, crossing fields before disappearing into the distance. All who saw this apparition believed it to be the ghost of a young boy who had been run down and killed by a train during the First World War.

This unfortunate boy was not the only supernatural entity that inhabited the hills and valleys of the north-west of England, especially Lancashire. A more terrifying one was that experienced by a signalman in his lonely cyrie at Entwistle. On many occasions he heard the dreaded eldritch cry of a boggart. It is this chilling cry which has earned the boggart its alternative name of 'shrieker', although in some parts of the north it goes by the other names such as 'barguest' or 'trash'. Regarded as an omen of death, the boggart usually takes the form of an enormous black or white dog, shaggy, fierce and with enormous staring eyes. Boggarts can take human form and are usually malevolent, but well-wishing boggarts were sometimes known to help out with tedious household chores. The rugged moors around Entwistle are excellent boggart country. The presence of these beings is remembered in the name of a public park in north Manchester called Boggart Hole Clough.

Entwistle Station on the Bolton to Blackburn line can be a bleak spot. The route was once busy enough to warrant quadruple tracks. Note the elevated signal box to give the signalman the best view of the tracks under his control.

Helmshore to Ramsbottom

The origin of the East Lancashire Railway lies with a line opened in 1846 linking Manchester to Bury via Clifton Junction and Radcliffe. This then proceeded along the Rossendale Valley through such delightful sounding places as Ramsbottom and Summerseat to Rawtenstall. An extension from Stubbins, just north of Ramsbottom, to Accrington, complete with ferocious gradients around Baxenden as steep as 1 in 38 and 1 in 40, was opened in 1848. The ELR was later absorbed by the Lancashire & Yorkshire Railway.

Mysterious happenings occurred on the southern stretch of this line between Helmshore and Ramsbottom in the late 1950s. The platelayers and gangers who maintained the track in those days were a tough lot, prepared to be out in all weathers and able to do heavy physical work as well as paying scrupulous attention to the state of the track, an attention which could make the vital difference between safety and disaster. They were also a close-knit lot, which didn't mean that they necessarily all got on well with each other!

Two of the men in the gang certainly seemed to have it in for each other. What had started as good-natured banter turned increasingly edgy with personal insults, and then degenerated further into fisticuffs. On several occasions the men had to be separated and prevented from doing serious injury to each other. This culminated in tragedy. The gang were checking a stretch of track between the stations when one of the men, some distance ahead of the others, found that the door of a platelayer's cabin was open. These little buildings contained tools and other equipment and made tempting targets for thieves.

He entered, whereupon he was followed in by another of the gang who dealt him such a blow on the head that it killed him instantly. The assailant was one of the men who were at loggerheads and he had mistaken the man who went into the cabin for the work-mate he so much hated.

It wasn't long before the scene of this tragedy gained the nickname 'The Murder Cabin'. Nor was it long before the ghost of the murdered man made his presence felt. The men came to call the spectre 'George', which was odd because that hadn't been his name when he was alive. The first time one of the gang encountered George was when he was forced to take shelter during a torrential thunderstorm. It certainly knows how to rain in this part of Lancashire! He sat on an old barrow waiting for the storm to ease when a man walked in who he recognised as George and went and stood in the furthest dark corner without saying a word. This was odd but it didn't particularly bother the ganger. The rain stopped and out came the sun. He got up and went outside, to be followed by the spectre which then simply vanished into thin air. He decided to keep his experience to himself in case his mates thought he was off his trolley. On another occasion the whole gang were crushed together in the cabin sheltering from a storm when the same figure walked in, passed through the press of bodies as if they weren't there and went to stand in the same dark corner. They all recognised George and scarcely batted an eyelid, knowing that he had the habit of returning to the scene of his death. It was clear that they all accepted George as the resident ghost.

Passenger services over this stretch of line ceased in 1966, the withdrawal of freight trains followed and the track was dismantled, some of the formation now being used by the A56 road. And that's progress?

LEICESTERSHIRE

Rothley

Rothley is one of the four stations on the restored Great Central Railway. The origins of the Great Central lie in a number of railway companies which amalgamated to form the Manchester, Sheffield & Lincolnshire Railway in 1847. This company was sometimes derided as the 'Money Sunk & Lost'. In fact the company developed its operations on a complicated network of lines cutting an east to west swathe from Cleethorpes through North Lincolnshire, South Yorkshire, into South Lancashire, Cheshire, Merseyside, as far as Wrexham in North Wales, sometimes by arrangements with other companies. The MS&L moved vast quantities of freight and mineral traffic, especially coal, over these lines.

In 1864 the company came under the chairmanship of Edward Watkin (later Sir Edward), a ruthless and ambitious entrepreneur who was not content with its provincial nature and was determined that it should have an extension to London. Even that wasn't enough because he then proposed that, via the lines of other companies he controlled, this route would be further extended to the Kent coast and, through a tunnel under the Channel, would connect his railway empire with various major cities on the Continent. A grand vision indeed!

Pushing aside those who argued that another line from the North to London wasn't needed, he launched the building of the 'London Extension' from near Annesley, north of Nottingham, through the latter city, Leicester and Rugby, to Quainton in Buckinghamshire and then, by arrangement with the Metropolitan Railway and a short piece of its own line, to a station in London at Marylebone. This new operation was to be called the 'Great Central Railway'.

The line was built on a magnificent scale, heavily engineered to mini-mise gradients. It was truly a high-speed route and, as further evidence of Watkin's grandiose scheme, it was built to accommodate continental rolling stock which has a more generous loading gauge than is normal in Britain. The story of its decline in the 1950s and '60s under the stewardship of British Railways has often been told and never fails to arouse emotions. Be that as it may, the bulk of the line was closed, although a residual service was kept from Rugby to Arkwright Street Station in Nottingham, this finally being withdrawn in 1969.

Rothley still sees trains because an eight-mile stretch from the northern sub-urbs of Leicester to Loughborough was restored and reopened by the Great Central Railway as a heritage line. Each of the four stations has a time theme, and Rothley's is the period shortly before the First World War. As well as provid-ing a delightful evocation of train travel in those far-off days, Rothley Station has acquired the reputation of being haunted. Ghosts present are said to include that of a former stationmaster who fusses about self-importantly marshalling passengers who, like him, are dressed in Edwardian fashions. The supporting cast includes very occasionally an aged, stooped man said to be a former signal-man, a young and very smart woman flourishing a parasol and a lady who is slightly anachronistic because she is dressed in Victorian modes.

LINCOLNSHIRE

Barkston

Barkston is a few miles north of Grantham and is the place where the East Coast Main Line crosses the Nottingham to Sleaford, Boston and Skegness route. There was formerly a triangular junction at Barkston, one side of which was a south to east curve allowing trains from Grantham to proceed directly to Skegness or, via Leadenham, to Lincoln. A north to east curve allowed trains from the Newark and Doncaster to access the Skegness line directly while the western side of the triangle was the East Coast Main Line. All these lines were built by the Great Northern Railway. Until 1955 there was a small station on the main line at the southern end of the triangle.

At one time locomotives fresh from building or repair at Doncaster Works would be given a gentle running-in by travelling from Doncaster, taking the north to east curve to Barkston East Junction, reversing from there to Barkston South Junction and then, facing north, returning to Doncaster where their drivers would report any faults that needed rectifying before the locomotives were given final clearance from the works. These locomotives might be from Scotland or the north-east of England, and some of them might not normally be seen so far south. This meant that the Barkston area attracted trainspotters eager to underline such exotic beasts in their dog-eared Ian Allan abcs. Trainspotters had much in common with twitchers.

At one time numerous reports were received of a mysterious figure that crossed the line perilously close to advancing trains and much to the annoyance and concern of their drivers. The same figure was also seen scaling the ladders up to the arms of the old-fashioned somersault semaphore signals as if to inspect the oil lamps to ensure they were functioning correctly. It was not unknown for trainspotters to do foolish things while showing off to their mates. Was this figure the ghost of some forgotten trainspotter re-enacting the foolhardy actions of the past? Or is there some other explanation? Trainspotters these days are far fewer in number. No one has seen the spectre of Barkston for nearly fifty years.

The East Coast Main Line and the Skegness line are still operational. The Barkston Junctions, however, are no more.

Bourne

Bourne is a pleasant small town in south Lincolnshire. It was once the junction of lines that radiated to all four cardinal points. The first of these was the Bourne & Essendine Railway which was opened in May 1860 and gave the town access to the route of the Great Northern Railway from London that became known as the East Coast Main Line. This company was absorbed by the Great Northern in 1864, and it enjoyed a slow and somnolent existence until 1951 when it closed completely. In August 1866 the Spalding & Bourne Railway opened and later became part of a company with greater ambitions, as suggested by its name: the Midland & Eastern Railway. In 1872 the Great Northern Railway opened its route to Sleaford from Bourne, this closing to passengers in 1930. The final opening was that in 1894 of the line to Little Bytham Junction and Saxby to the west. This and the line eastwards to Spalding became part of the Midland & Great Northern Joint Railway and its fabled cross-country route from the Norfolk coast to the East Midlands.

Many existing buildings were taken over and adapted for railway use in Britain in the nineteenth century, and one of the most interesting is Red Hall at Bourne. Although the origins of the hall are not absolutely certain, it is thought to have been built around 1600 and almost certainly by a member of the local Fisher dynasty. Later on in the seventeenth century it came into the hands of the Digby family. This has led to the emergence of a local myth which has almost taken on the status of received wisdom. This avers that the Red Hall has a connection with the family of Sir Everard Digby, one of the chief conspirators in the Gunpowder Plot of 1605. The myth has shamelessly been expanded by those who say that Red Hall was one of the meeting points of the conspirators while they were planning their dastardly deed. Never letting the truth get in the way of a good story, it has even been alleged that Red Hall is haunted by the ghosts of some of the gunpowder plotters!

In 1857 Red Hall was sold to the Bourne & Essendine Railway Co. It was within a few yards of the railway and it became a rather grand stationmaster's house and ticket office. It later came under the ownership of the M&GN Railway who decided that it was no longer suitable for their purposes and it was proposed for demolition. This suggestion created an absolute furore in the town, and the locals, with the assistance of the Society for the Protection of Ancient Buildings, were successful in preventing the demolition from going ahead.

Passenger trains ceased at Bourne in February 1959 when large parts of the M&GN lost their passenger and in some cases all their services, closing completely. Freight services were withdrawn from the town in 1965. Red Hall became redundant when passenger trains finished and its condition was allowed to deteriorate until once more it became a candidate for demolition. Fortunately in 1962 it was acquired by the Bourne United Charities and, with the aid of various grants, an expensive repair and refurbishment was done. It then became a community resource greatly appreciated by the townsfolk.

One of the authors used to present courses for the Workers' Educational Association in a room in Red Hall. One particular course was held on ten winter evenings, and on those occasions a key-holder would appear a few minutes before the meetings were due to start in order to open the building up. The author liked to prowl around the grassy area surrounding the hall, even in the dark, and to speculate about what the place must have been like when there was considerable railway activity so close by. He remembers very clearly his surprise when one night he arrived about half an hour early and found the door open but no lights on in the building. Deliberately not turning the lights on, he decided to have a look at the rooms upstairs. They were very atmospheric in the almost total darkness, but not threatening in any way. There was nobody about. He made his way back down to the room on the ground floor where the meetings took place, still with ten or so minutes to spare. He remembers even more clearly how he then heard the clear and unmistakeable sound of creaking floorboards as someone moved around in one of the upstairs rooms. The key-holder was amazed to find him installed because the hall had been left locked. Was it a human intruder or someone from the 'other side' in Red Hall that winter's evening?

Front of Red Hall, Bourne. Few main station buildings in small country towns were located in such distinguished premises.

Red Hall from the south.

Claxby & Usselby

This station served two settlements with strong Scandinavian origins as indicated in the '-by' element in their names. As so often happened, the station was not located very conveniently for either of them. It was on the line originally built by the Manchester, Sheffield & Lincolnshire Railway (later the Great Central) from Lincoln through Market Rasen to Barnetby and Grimsby, and it opened for business in 1848.

In the 1960s tragedy struck in the signal box when the signalman on duty suffered a sudden and fatal heart attack. Subsequently other men working in the box heard a variety of strange and inexplicable noises which included a disembodied voice. What sent shivers through them was the fact that they knew the voice. It was unmistakable. It was that of their deceased colleague!

The line is still operational but the station closed in March 1960.

Elsham

Elsham was a small wayside station on what became the line of the Manchester, Sheffield & Lincolnshire Railway (later Great Central Railway) between Doncaster, Barnetby and Grimsby. This stretch of line was opened in 1866. Close to where the line crosses the Ancholme River an accident occurred in the 1920s in which four people were killed. Fog in Britain is not what it used to be, but during the period from 1930 to the 1950s there were strange reports that on those occasions when a fog descended an eerie stationary steam locomotive could be seen, the fiery glow from its furnace visible from afar. No one

Elsham; a typical wayside station of the former Manchester, Sheffield & Lincolnshire Railway, known to many as the 'Money, Sunk and Lost' railway!

has claimed a sighting since. The line through the former Elsham Station is still operational.

French Drove

The line from Spalding to March was built by the Great Northern Railway Co. and opened in 1867. In 1882 it became part of the Great Northern & Great Eastern Joint Railway Co. The line, for all that it passed through the heart of the rural Lincolnshire Fens, was a very heavily used major goods and mineral route, part of a system joining the coal-producing districts of west and south Yorkshire and Nottinghamshire to the coal-starved districts of East Anglia and, more particularly, London.

French Drove Station had had a period when it was known as French Drove and Gedney Hill. The latter part of the name is a commentary on the relative nature of language. Any piece of land protruding more than a couple of feet above the extraordinarily uniform flatness of the Fens constitutes a hill in these parts. The station closed to passenger traffic in September 1961 and the station house was put on the market. A family from outside the district moved in, and they were slightly nonplussed when a local postmistress told them in no uncertain terms that the house they had moved into was haunted.

The family was a level-headed lot, not taking this kind of information too seriously. However, it wasn't long before strange occurrences were happening in their new home. This they were renovating themselves, the house needing a lot of work to make it liveable in. Their mail was usually delivered by a post lady on a bicycle. One morning they had made an early start and were beavering away busily when they heard a woman's voice by the front door, which they often left open on warm days. They assumed that it was the friendly post lady and one of them went to greet her. No one was there. No post either – it came later that day. This was puzzling, but the woman's voice was soon forgotten as they buckled down to work again.

A few weeks later a youngish man knocked on their door. He told them that he had worked at the station a few years ago, was revisiting the area and had to come to have a look for sentimental reasons, and was curious as to who was occupying the house now that passengers no longer came and went – not that there'd been many in the latter years, anyway. He was very pleasant and they invited him in for a cup of tea. He had plenty of memories of the old days and kept them interested, but they certainly pricked up their ears when he told them that many years previously a stationmaster had hanged himself in the room above the former ticket office. His wife used to help out by closing the station at night, and when it was dark she attended to these duties carrying a lantern because the station, like so many others in the depths of the countryside, was ill-lit. She herself hadn't been able to face life without her husband, and she simply lost the will to live, withered away and died not long after his death. The man told them that a figure carrying a lamp was often seen in the vicinity of the station during the hours of darkness, which is why many of the locals avoided going anywhere near the place if at all possible. Everyone felt that the place was haunted.

This revelation inevitably had a slightly dampening effect on their enthusiasm for the building and renovation work they were doing on the house. This feeling became much stronger a few months later when, last thing at night, one of the family spotted what looked like a lamp being carried along the formation of the old line, 100 yards or so away. He called the others who all agreed about what they saw. A few restless nights followed until they discovered that it was actually the lamp on the bike belonging to a man who lived in a former crossing-keeper's cottage a mile or two down the line and who used often to take a shortcut home where once the trains had thundered past at all hours of the day and night.

This still left the mystery of the woman's voice early that morning and the tales of apparitions around the old station so gloatingly repeated by the locals.

The late Sir John Betjeman neatly captured the feeling of the Fens at night with these lines from *A Lincolnshire Tale* in his *New Bats in Old Belfries* published in 1945:

The remoteness was awful, the stillness intense,
Of invisible fenland, around and immense;

The line through French Drove which once witnessed the romantic boat train that ran from Harwich Parkeston Quay to Liverpool suffered as the volume of coal and general freight traffic on the railways declined in the 1970s. The boat train itself was diverted away to travel via Peterborough and Nottingham in 1973, and the rot then really set in, the local passenger services between March and Spalding being withdrawn in 1982. The last freight trains followed not long after.

Grantham

A horrific accident occurred at Grantham on a September night in 1906. An Anglo-Scottish express conveying sleeping carriages, ordinary passenger accommodation and some parcel-vans had left King's Cross at 20.45 and called only at Peterborough where a relief footplate crew and fresh locomotive took over. It was a calm and clear night, the train was on time and the two men on the footplate were known to be steady and conscientious. The locomotive was a large-boilered Great Northern Ivatt Atlantic, No.276, which was a 'good-un' and in tip-top mechanical condition. The next scheduled stop was Grantham, about thirty-five minutes away.

The station staff at Grantham were making ready for the train's arrival and a handful of passengers were standing waiting, poised, if at all possible, to find empty compartments and compose themselves for undisturbed sleep. To the consternation of all on the platform, the train entered the platform road at a speed of about 40mph, clearly with no intention of stopping. Consternation quickly turned to horror and dread as the train took the turn-out for the Nottingham line and then a reverse curve. The tender derailed, hitting the parapet of a bridge and making a sound like an explosion followed by a sickening and never-to-be-forgotten series of crunching and wrenching noises as the rest of the train piled up behind it. Some of the carriages tumbled down the embankment and caught fire. Even the carriages left on the track ignited as burning coal from the firebox flew in all directions. They were, of course, all wooden-bodied in those days. Driver and fireman, eleven passengers and a postal sorter lost their lives.

No satisfactory explanation for the accident was ever given in spite of the usual scrupulous inquiry and report. The signals at the north end of the platform were at danger to allow a goods train from the Nottingham direction to have the road onto the Peterborough line, crossing the path of the Anglo-Scottish express. The distant signal protecting these points had correctly been set at caution, but the express, which all the witnesses said had not applied its brakes, went through the danger signals and then fatally took the tracks to Nottingham. These points were of course interlocked with those from the Nottingham direction, and were not intended to be taken at such a speed, but it was almost certainly the following reverse curve that caused the train to derail with such disastrous consequences. 'Explanations' varied from the driver and fireman mistaking where they were as the train approached Grantham, driver and fireman engaged in a fight to the death on the footplate, and one or other of them suddenly being taken ill and his mate going to assist him. All these were rendered unlikely given the evidence of the signalman in Grantham South signal box, that when the train passed him both men were correctly at their posts on either side of the footplate observing the line ahead through the windows in the front of the locomotive's cab. When all possible explanations had been eliminated, the impossible kicked in and there were suggestions that the driver and fireman had been mesmerised by the appearance of a ghost. The exact truth about the accident at Grantham will never be known.

About twenty years later a keen student of locomotive performance caught a train from London to York. The locomotive was the old 276, now renumbered as LNER 3276. It was a very undistinguished run and the train was about ten minutes late into York. It was not scheduled to stop at Grantham and the observer was very puzzled by the fact that the train slowed to little more than 20mph as it passed through Grantham, even though all the signals were clear. At York he spoke to the driver and asked him why he had proceeded so slowly through Grantham. The driver unblushingly told him that 3276 was a jinxed locomotive and with that particular day being the anniversary of the Grantham smash, he had taken no chances just in case the engine decided to take the

Grantham Station looking south. The accident occurred on the curve behind the photographer.

wrong road once more. No drivers or firemen mourned the day that No.3276 went off to be scrapped at Doncaster Works.

Grimsby

In its heyday, Grimsby was probably the largest fishing port in the world. It owed its importance to the railways. In 1845 parliamentary authority was given to proposals for a number of lines in north Lincolnshire which would link up with a projected line to Sheffield. These lines went on to become part of the Manchester, Sheffield & Lincolnshire Railway, and this in turn became the Great Central Railway. The other company that gained rail access to Grimsby was the Great Northern, and this was by means of the East Lincolnshire line from Peterborough through Spalding, Boston and Louth. The MS&LR opened the first fish dock at Grimsby in 1856. By the 1890s Grimsby was handling a quarter of all the rail-borne fish traffic in England and Wales. In conjunction with the development of steam-powered trawlers, the railways effected a huge improvement in the diet of the British working class because they made fresh fish relatively cheap and available across the whole of the country.

Trains of special vans for the fresh fish traffic were marshalled in sidings between Grimsby and Cleethorpes. These trains were continuously braked so that they could run at the high speed which was necessary given the perishable nature of the payload, the brakes of course being controlled by the driver in the locomotive. For the brakes to work, the vacuum pipes of all the wagons had to be carefully connected to each other and that on the leading van to the locomotive's tender. The problem was that a section of the sidings where these trains were made up developed a sinister reputation in the 1950s, so much so that some men refused to work in them on the night shift.

The following is an example of the kind of thing that happened all too frequently. One night the shunter had connected up all the pipes, working as quickly as he could because he never liked the atmosphere in this part of the yard. He could never quite put his finger on why he had this feeling. On this particular night it seemed more menacing than ever. When the driver tested the pressure, it was evident that one or more of the vacuum pipes on the vans were not properly connected. Another shunter went along the train and couldn't find any problem. Still the pressure was way below that required. The engine driver was getting impatient as the time for departure was looming, and these trains were tightly timed. A third shunter volunteered to examine the connections, and as he left the comforting presence of the others he felt as if there was some unseen and malevolent being ready to waylay him. This feeling became stronger and stronger, and it did not help when the light in his powerful torch started flickering and then dimmed. His sense that something sinister was there was bad enough, but then an awful stench assailed his nostrils. It was the stench of bodily corruption. He could not find anything amiss with the connections and he made his way back, almost running, such was his state of mind. The driver checked the vacuum for the third time. The pressure hadn't changed. By now the driver was hopping mad and he gave the shunters a piece of his mind. They then agreed that he would lead them all for one final check. If there was anything wrong they would find it this time. They had to do so or the train would be late leaving and questions would be asked. With a marked lack of enthusiasm they followed him using their torches to probe the baleful darkness. All the torches flickered and dimmed at the same spot, and then came the smell. Even the driver was affected by the sense of evil; the others were literally sweating and shaking with fear. However, the driver found a loose connection which he quickly put right and they all got out of that loathsome place, quite unashamedly running in order to do so.

Some years later a man committed suicide exactly at the spot where the sense of evil was strongest. When it was dark in the sidings, he knelt down and placed his neck on the track. His head was severed as the wheels of a van passed over it. Was there a connection?

Unfortunately no fresh fish traffic now goes by rail. The line between Grimsby and Cleethorpes is still operational.

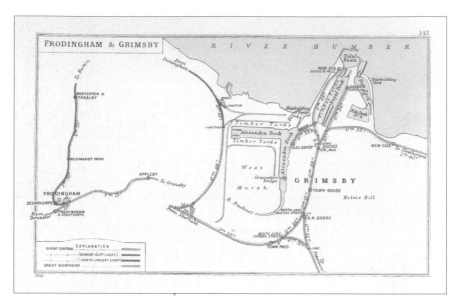

The haunted sidings for fish traffic were between Grimsby Docks and New Clee Station.

Hallington

The line of the Great Northern Railway from Louth to Bardney went through the heart of the Lincolnshire Wolds. It traversed some remote and beautiful country-side which even in the twenty-first century remains comparatively little-known. It was not very promising territory for a railway, even in the headily optimistic days of the mid-nineteenth century, and the building of the 971-yard-long Withcall Tunnel proved particularly troublesome. The line was sanctioned in 1866 but not opened until 1876. It did not earn enough even to pay the interest on the capital borrowed to build it! In 1883 it was bought by the Great Northern Railway, a trifle unwillingly, at a knockdown price. They didn't really know what to do with it. It slumbered on providing a useful service for a smattering of local people and being of assistance to the farming communities of this part of Lincolnshire, but the passenger trains were withdrawn as early as November 1951. Goods trains lingered on for a few years but eventually succumbed to the inevitable.

Hallington is one of several locations in the UK where people claim to have heard the ghostly sound of steam trains puffing through the night many years after services ceased. The sound of a steam locomotive hard at work is pretty unmistakeable. How is it to be explained?

Hibaldstow Crossing

Scawby and Hibaldstow was a wayside station on the line of the former Manchester, Sheffield & Lincolnshire Railway (later Great Central Railway)

A few miles west of Hallington Station was Withcall where the line passed under the Lincolnshire Wolds in a tunnel over half a mile long. This is lonely country and it takes little imagination to hear a ghost train's shrieking whistle as it emerges from this forbidding tunnel.

from Cleethorpes and Grimsby through Brigg, Gainsborough, Retford and Worksop to Sheffield, completed in 1849.

Just north-east of the station, which was mid-way between the two villages it served, a minor road crossed the railway on the flat, and there the railway company built a gatekeeper's cabin with a small cottage adjacent. Manning this crossing meant a lonely vigil, particularly at night. Emerging every so often from the relative cosiness of the cabin on a wet or freezing night to open and close the gates was not everybody's idea of the best way to earn a crust. Hibaldstow Crossing was a bleak and exposed spot.

In the middle of the 1920s the regular crossing-keeper was off work due to illness and his duties were being temporarily covered by a porter deputed from Scawby and Hibaldstow Station. What on the face of it appeared to be a simple task, that of opening and closing the crossing gates in response to indicators from the signal boxes on either side saying that a train was approaching, in reality required alertness and adroit timing. Unfortunately the stand-in crossing-keeper was not up to the job and he was knocked down and killed by a train while opening the gates – unfortunately for him, not quickly enough.

It seems that the unfortunate man may have died and been buried but his spirit could not tear itself away from the scene of his death. Subsequent crossing-keepers came to hate night duty at Hibaldstow Crossing because their shifts were often interrupted by the sound of very measured footsteps approaching and passing their lonely little cabin. Those men intrepid enough to emerge to issue a challenge were made to look stupid because nothing was ever to be seen. The other men who were understandably reluctant to leave their little haven to investigate the darkness outside looked like simple cowards. These noises were heard on many occasions and by many different men, and the only explanation they had was that the footsteps were those of the ghost of the unfortunate temporary crossing-keeper.

Scawby and Hibaldstow Station closed in 1968 and the 'haunted' crossing nearby was converted to automatic barriers in 1966, but the line through this area, while still operating, could with justification be described as a 'ghost railway'. This line, almost incredibly, only operates on Saturdays with three trains in each direction stopping at the remaining intermediate stations of Brigg, Kirton Lindsey and Gainsborough Central. Attempts to close the line in the late 1980s aroused ferocious protests, but when, in 1991, all the other trains were withdrawn and this derisory service was introduced, little or nothing was said. A passenger who missed the last train to Cleethorpes on a Saturday would have to wait seven nights and six days for the next train. In the cold comfort of a bus shelter masquerading as a railway station, this would indeed be a long wait.

Tallington

There is a busy level crossing at Tallington where the A16 crosses the East Coast Main Line close to the southern extremity of Lincolnshire. The signaller in the box which controls the crossing can make himself immensely unpopular when he gives precedence to what can sometimes be a long succession of trains on this impressive stretch of quadruple track and equally impressive queues of impatient road-users build up. The station at this point closed in 1959.

This location is reputedly haunted by the ghost of a man who jumped off the old footbridge. The ghost appears on the anniversary of this event, thought to be 15 January. His wife had died and the poor fellow simply couldn't handle life on his own.

MERSEYSIDE

James Street

Railway passenger services under the River Mersey between James Street, Liverpool, and Hamilton Square, Birkenhead, began in 1886. Short extensions were soon made at either end. Before the tunnel existed, those wanting to travel between the Wirral and Liverpool and vice versa were forced to take a ferry. The river could be distinctly choppy, the wind cold and strong enough to knock the unwary off their feet, and an impenetrable and damp fog might blanket the river and cause delays as the constant sound of invisible ships' sirens boomed out, warning of the hazards lying in wait for the ferry which perforce had to cross the shipping lanes virtually at right angles.

The trains were much quicker and were not affected by climatic conditions, but in the early years the Mersey Railway was steam-operated. The locomotives had to be powerful enough to drag themselves and their carriages up gradients as steep as 1 in 27. They were supposed to consume their own smoke and condense their steam, but in practice they turned the atmosphere in subterranean stations like James Street and Hamilton Square into something so oppressive that travellers rediscovered their loyalty to the ferries. Freezing in fresh air on the ferries seemed preferable to subterranean near-asphyxiation. However, in 1903 the loss-making Mersey Railway was electrified. It became the first railway in Britain to be entirely converted from steam to electric multiple-unit operation. The problem was that travellers from place like Rock Ferry, Wallasey and West Kirby, served by the Wirral Railway, had to put up with the inconvenience of changing trains to join the Mersey Railway for the quick run under the river.

The possibility of electrifying the Wirral Railway network was voiced time and time again, but the 1920s and '30s were not good times for many areas of Britain's economy, including that of Merseyside. Eventually the Government made money available for capital projects to try to kick start the economy. Work on the electrification started in 1936 and the Wirral and Mersey parts of what was then the London Midland & Scottish Railway were integrated. The very modernistic and comfortable electric trains began running in March 1938. People living in the northern end of the Wirral must have thought all their birthdays had come at once.

In the 1950s two young people, a boy and his girlfriend, had been celebrating St Valentine's Day by visiting two or three pubs in the city centre of Liverpool. They felt pleasantly relaxed as they made their way to James Street Station to catch their train back to Leasowe in the Wirral. They descended to the platform and sat down, noticing a woman sitting on another bench nearby. She was certainly rather noticeable. She was dressed in curiously old-fashioned clothes, but somehow managed to be elegant because of the obvious quality of the clothes she was wearing and also because of the way she wore them. She sat stock-still, seemingly preoccupied by her thoughts. The train arrived and the lady and the young couple got into the same carriage, it being empty of other passengers. All three sat down, the woman a couple of bays away. The train doors slid closed and the train moved off along the tunnel under the murky waters of the Mersey. Just before Hamilton Square the couple looked up. The woman had vanished. Except for themselves, the carriage was absolutely empty!

The lad even got up and walked the length of the carriage. They knew they were not mistaken — the woman had got on with them and had disappeared

The Water Street entrance to James Street Station on the underground section of the Mersey Railway sported this delightful sign advertising its electric trains which ran under the Mersey from Liverpool to the Cheshire shore at Birkenhead. The line is now part of Merseyrail.

into thin air. For years after they would ponder over the events of that night. What was the story behind the disappearing woman? Had they seen a ghost?

Trains still run under the Mersey, but the new generation of electric multiple units do not have the same style or comfort as the solid rolling stock of the late 1930s.

Walton Junction

'Walton Junction' is a curious name for this station because it is not, nor has it ever been, a junction. It is, however, in the Walton district of north-east Liverpool. It is on a line promoted by the Liverpool, Ormskirk & Preston Railway, work on the building of which started in 1847. It eventually came to be part of the empire of the Lancashire & Yorkshire Railway. The line is still operational, being part of the Merseyrail network as far as Ormskirk.

1968 was the last year of the regular use of steam locomotives on the standard-gauge lines of British Railways, and virtually all the remaining 'steamers' were concentrated in the north-west of England. They were a pretty woebegone lot by this time. They suffered from little maintenance and less cleaning, but the steam locomotive is a rugged machine and somehow they maintained a certain dignity even in their last gasps. They may have been run-down but they were still fascinating machines to watch, and many people were only too aware that their removal from the scene represented a historic watershed. They were a direct link with the Industrial Revolution and the coal, iron and heavy manufacturing industries which had been so dominant when Britain was 'the workshop of the world'. De-industrialisation was changing the face of the country and the lives of the people, and not everyone was sure that it was for the good. Meanwhile, tens of thousands of railway enthusiasts descended on the north-west of England to see steam playing out its last painful months.

In the mid-1960s a Liverpool man used to take his son to Walton Junction to watch the few remaining steam trains. For the young lad, excitement at the prospect of seeing a 'steamer' was tempered by the horrible feelings of fear he always got when reaching a certain point on the path beside the railway line. He always felt that something malevolent was watching him, but he was afraid to tell his dad. In 1975 he returned to Walton Junction and walked along the self-same path, this time with two friends. During the intervening years it had become rather more unkempt and the young man, for that is what he now was, remembered the past but thought that the fear he had always encountered was perhaps nothing more than a childish whimsy. He told them nothing of the feelings he used to experience at this spot and was amazed when both his friends said they felt something nasty in the place. They said it was as if they were being watched by someone or something evil. Shortly afterwards the three young men returned, this time with a girl making up the party. They told her nothing, but likewise she said that she felt something dangerous and couldn't wait to get away.

When the man had children of his own, he made yet another return to Walton Junction and he walked the familiar footpath, now even more ramshackle, with them. They didn't seem to sense anything untoward, but he realised that he was marshalling them along the footpath as quickly as possible and constantly looking over his shoulder – for what? Close to the station was a row of cottages that once used to house railway workers and their families. Occupied the last time he had been there, they were now a sad and derelict eyesore. Unwanted and empty, they were waiting for the demolition men. With the children he stood and gazed at the cottages for a moment when suddenly there was a loud bang from the back of one of them, a bang as if someone had slammed a door using excessive force. Now he had an awful reprise of his childish feelings of horror. Gathering the children together, he hurried away with no backward glances. He hasn't been back to Walton Junction since then but he often wonders what it is that spooks the place. He only has to think 'Walton Junction' and the hairs rise on the back of his neck.

This station, now called Walton (Merseyside), used to be called Walton Junction, which is odd because it never was a junction.

NORFOLK

Abbey and West Dereham

East Anglia had several extremely rustic branch lines. 'Twigs' rather than branches might have been a more appropriate word. One such was the line from Denver to Stoke Ferry. Although it was built by the obscure Downham & Stoke Ferry Railway Co., the line was always operated by the Great Eastern Railway and fully absorbed by it on 1 January 1898. It had opened in 1882 and was built primarily to serve the farming community. The line lost its meagre passenger service in 1930. Freight traffic ceased in the mid-1960s, and the line was soon ripped up.

A couple who lived at West Dereham had a strange experience in the 1950s. By this time freight trains ran only 'as required', which wasn't very often, and so they were surprised to be woken up by the sound of a train in the middle of the night. To their amazement, they could see that it was a passenger train composed of a steam locomotive and two carriages with their compartments lit up. It was 3.00 in the morning. Even in its heyday, and it never really had one, no passenger trains ran on the line at that hour and, anyway, passenger services had been withdrawn about twenty-five years previously. As the sound of the train petered out into the distance, they scratched and pinched themselves and asked whether

The rather stylish frontage of Norwich Station was built in 1886. This station used to be called Norwich (Thorpe) to distinguish it from three other stations that used to serve the city. There is no sign of the Norwich Station horror.

they had been seeing things. None the wiser for their ruminations, they eventually returned to bed and sleep. The man told his workmates about the train the next morning and they just laughed. By now seriously confused, the couple went down to the railway that evening. Weeds were growing on the track; a signal post leant at a crazy angle; everything looked semi-derelict. What is more, there was a thick coating of rust on the rails. It was obvious that no train had passed for weeks. What did the couple see that night from their window in West Dereham?

NORTH YORKSHIRE

Middlesborough

Middlesborough owes its existence to the railway. The Stockton & Darlington Railway was opened in 1825 with the purpose of conveying coal from the pits of south-west Durham to the River Tees at Stockton. The river at Stockton proved difficult to navigate for the large collier vessels and so what would now be called a 'greenfield site', located by deeper water, was chosen, and the S&D was extended to it in 1830. This was the origin of Middlesborough. The town grew with extraordinary rapidity as it became a major industrial centre with iron and steel-making and extensive docks. In 1831 the population was 383; in 1841 5,709; 1881 56,000 and in 1911 109,000.

All the lines in the Middlesborough area came under the control of the North Eastern Railway, who rebuilt the station in 1877 in the then fashionable neo-Gothic style. In a town not noted for buildings of particular architectural merit, it is one of the best, and it looked even more distinctive when it still had its fine overall-roof.

Walking to start his shift one afternoon in the 1950s, a young railwayman saw a figure approaching and as he got closer he recognised him as a signalman with

Middlesborough's Victorian
Gothic station interior.

Middlesborough
Station at
platform level.
Making up in
height for what
it lacks in beauty
is the overall
roof, which was
destroyed in an
air raid during
the Second World
War.

whom he was on friendly terms. He was about 20 yards away and just about to utter some kind of greeting when the signalman vanished. There was no cover or anything he could have hidden behind. The signalman was simply there one moment and gone the next. The younger man went on his way feeling confused and puzzled. Imagine how these feelings intensified when his workmates told him there had been a tragedy earlier in the day. A signalman had been run down by a train and killed. The signalman was the same man who had walked towards him and then vanished only a few minutes previously.

The line through Middlesborough is still operational.

Sandsend

The line from Whitby to Loftus was authorised in 1866 and construction work by the Whitby, Redcar & Middlesborough Union Railway started in 1871. A host of problems afflicted the construction of the line and it did not open until 1884. It was absorbed by the North Eastern Railway in 1889 and closed in 1958. It offered superb views of the coast, especially at Staithes, Kettleness and Sandsend. The line had to cross the valleys carved by streams rising on the moors to the west just before they tumbled into the sea, and it did so by means of spectacular iron viaducts, the largest of which was at Staithes. The exposed nature of this particular viaduct caused it to be fitted with a wind gauge, and when gusts reached a certain

The railway in Sandsend, running from Whitby to Loftus along the cliff top behind the houses on the left, crossed the beck on a lofty viaduct and plunged into the tunnel in the cliffs in the distance. This was one of Britain's most scenic lines.

speed, a bell rang in the signal box at Staithes and trains would not be allowed over the viaduct until the winds abated.

The tunnel at Sandsend is 1,652 yards long and has gained the reputation of being haunted. Phenomena that have allegedly been seen include white lights, figures of people who seem to be able to melt away through the wall when approached, footsteps without anyone to make them and the whistle of a steam train.

NOTTINGHAMSHIRE

Burton Joyce

In 1844 the Midland Railway was created from a merger of the Midland Counties, the North Midland and the Birmingham & Derby Junction railway companies. The Midland became a major player on the national railway scene. The merger was the brainchild of the energetic, ambitious and ruthless George Hudson, one of the first, and later one of the most infamous, of the Victorian railway moguls. He built spheres of influence like the territories of an empire. He feared that what he considered as part of his fiefdom, the control of the two existing routes from York to London via Derby, was threatened by proposals to build one or more direct lines from York to London by routes considerably further east. Trying to pre-empt such a development, unsuccessfully as it happened, he built a long cross-country line from Nottingham to Lincoln via Newark-on-Trent. This line opened in 1846 and Burton Joyce, a few miles east of Nottingham, was one of the small wayside stations.

Burton Joyce Station is on the southern extremity of the village, very close to the River Trent. About thirty years ago a signalman at Burton Joyce found many of his shifts disturbed by the sound of footsteps coming along the track and then ascending the steps to his small signal box. Whenever he looked out of the box or went to the door and opened it, he never managed to see who or what it was that was making the sounds. Understandably, he felt very uneasy about these disconcerting experiences and could not decide whether to have a chat with his fellow signalmen about it or tell the inspector who appeared at the box from time to time. After all it was not a good idea for a signalman to suggest by word or act that he was seeing things – not if he wanted to keep his job, that is. Fortunately he never did the ten at night to six in the morning shift, but he was considering asking for a transfer when, one shift following another in quick succession, he came to realise that the noises which he had dreaded coming to hear had stopped. We will never know whether they were a manifestation of the restless spirit of someone perhaps killed on the line around Burton Joyce or some thoughtless prankster oblivious to the dangers of spooking someone in a position of trust and responsibility like a railway signalman. The Nottingham to Lincoln is still operational.

Mechanical signal boxes have survived repeated notices of their imminent demise and, although they are greatly reduced in numbers in the twenty-first century, a sizeable number of these anachronistic installations still exist, especially away from the lines carrying the heaviest traffic and the fastest trains. Although those who work in signal boxes are now called signallers, and there are women among their number, this book, dealing essentially with the past, will continue to call them signalmen. Hopefully this will not cause offence.

It requires a very special kind of person to cope with the demands of the job. There are many failsafe devices to assist his operations, although the signalman still needs to be steady, systematic and extremely vigilant. The requirements of the job embrace other qualities. Many signal boxes were to be found in remote spots in the depth of the countryside, and night shifts in these boxes were not for those who possessed faint hearts or too lurid an imagination. The immense darkness on certain nights; the noises of the creatures of the night as they scuttled around their beats; the bark of the fox and the call of the owl could all play havoc with man's primeval fears. Often signal boxes were located in cuttings where the sense of remoteness could be almost tangible, and the animal noises did little to offset a feeling of all-enveloping silence. Even the presence of a country by-road some distance away, with the sound of an occasional car becoming even more occasional in the witching hours, somehow only served to emphasise the loneliness of the signalman's post.

Then, of course, in the days of the steam railways there were the trains themselves. In the hours of darkness steam trains immediately assumed an aura of mystery, both romantic and yet also rather sinister; somewhat threatening. Smoke from the chimney was illuminated by the glare from the firebox, and as the locomotive passed, a glimpse of the men on the footplate, the driver peering into the darkness, straining to catch the small, unblinking stare of the old semaphore signals, the fireman heaving coal into the hungry maw of the firebox. More types of train were around in those days. Express passenger trains went past with a rush and a roar, occasional glimpses of snug-looking compartments made cosy by steam heating; and even faster than the passenger expresses might be the milk trains rushing their perishable cargo up to London, or the fully braked fish trains from the likes of Grimsby. Even in the still of the night, the fish trains had their own unique olfactory way of marking their passage. Hurrying parcel trains and lumbering goods and mineral trains would be signalled on their way. Meat, livestock and mail trains all passed in the night. On many lines there were more trains about between ten in the evening and six in the morning than during daytime hours.

Even the interior of the signal box seemed mysterious; the lighting was deliberately made to be dim, and what light there was focussed on the block instruments and the train register in which the movements of all trains as well as any untoward events were recorded. The further corners of the box became at night places of dim surmise, odd flickers of movement perhaps reflecting a sudden flare-up from the coal in the well-stoked stove. In the event of a big storm with thunder and lightning, the block instruments clicked as if they were possessed by invisible spirits, and little blue sparks flew as the bells rang. It was once said that a signalman's job combined the worst features of the work of a lighthouse-keeper, the captain of a warship, the coxswain of a lifeboat and a night-watchman.

Mapperley Tunnel

Nottingham was one of many localities where bitter rivalries were fought out between railway companies vying with each other for access to sources of lucrative traffic. Here the main contenders were the Great Northern and Midland railways. Lesser players were the London & North Western and later the Great Central. The idea of transporting as much of the abundant 'black gold' as possible from the rich coalfields of Nottinghamshire and Derbyshire attracted these companies like a pot of jam attracts flies.

In the 1870s the Great Northern opened a line skirting round the eastern fringe of Nottingham, from Colwick, which led, eventually with extensions, through the heart of the coalfield in the Leen Valley to Newstead and on to Langwith Junction, and also to Pinxton, Heanor, Derby, Burton-on-Trent and even Stafford. On the eastern section of this system, through Gedling to Daybrook, hilly terrain was encountered, and the Great Northern was forced to bore through this with Mapperley Tunnel. This tunnel caused the railway civil engineers enormous headaches over the years on account of subsidence caused by mining. In 1925 part of the roof collapsed and in the late 1950s much of the roof had to be shored up with timber. The cost of making the tunnel good eventually became prohibitive and traffic was diverted away to alternative routes. Most of the line closed in April 1960. A stub from Netherfield to Gedling remains in situ at the time of writing (December 2008) although the connection at Netherfield to the line from Nottingham to Grantham has been severed.

In the 1970s a number of children playing near the south entrance to Mapperley Tunnel claim to have heard a steam train approaching them through the tunnel despite the fact that the rails had long since been lifted and it had been sealed at its northern end.

Netherfield has its own railway ghost – a man who walks the tracks from time to time and, when challenged, just disappears.

Rolleston

This station is on the same line as Burton Joyce (above). For a little station (long since unstaffed) there is a lot of paranormal activity. It includes a man who was knocked down and killed by a train who revisits the spot, a man reading a newspaper while he waits for a train but who then disappears before the train arrives, and bells ringing in a crossing-keeper's cottage to announce the approach of a train that never gets there.

Although the line was still busy, subsidence in Mapperley Tunnel meant that it had to be closed.

A delightful wayside station with steep gables, now a private house in Thurgarton – shame about the extension! The station is still served by trains on the Nottingham to Lincoln line. The ghostly sounds of children playing have been heard by the level crossing.

The station was formerly the junction for the Midland Railway branch line to Southwell and Mansfield. The short stub from Rolleston to Southwell outlasted the line on to Mansfield, but it closed to passengers in 1959. Southwell is one of the East Midland's little-known and hidden gems. It has a delightful Minster (actually a cathedral) with a fine Norman nave, unique western towers capped by 'Rhenish helms' and a chapter house with naturalistic carvings of sufficient quality to drive the austere art historian Sir Niklaus Pevsner into raptures of joy.

Down the line towards Burton Joyce is Thurgarton where a crossing-keeper's cottage was supposedly haunted by the sound of children at play. The manned crossing has been replaced by automatic lifting barriers.

OXFORDSHIRE

Shipton-on-Cherwell

On Christmas Eve 1874 a heavily loaded passenger train bound for Birkenhead was heading north from Oxford on the Great Western Railway's main line to Banbury. It had just passed Woodstock Road Station (later renamed Kidlington) when a piece of the metal tyre of the coach behind the locomotive came away, pulling the coach off the rails, although it stayed more-or-less upright. The train was double-headed, and when the drivers realised there was something amiss they made an emergency brake application. This slowed the train so drastically that couplings broke and nine carriages not only left the rails but tumbled down the embankment, piling up on either side of the frozen Oxford Canal, which the railway crossed at this point, close to the hamlet of Shipton-on-Cherwell. Thirty-four passengers died and nearly seventy received serious injuries.

Kidlington is a kind of outer-Oxford suburb, less than a mile from the scene of the accident. Back in the 1970s a perfectly ordinary-looking house in Kidlington was the scene of many inexplicable phenomena. These included activities often associated with the presence of a poltergeist, such as lights going on and off apparently of their own accord, doors opening and shutting likewise and sounds from unoccupied rooms – unoccupied that is by living people. Strong smells of burning were evident on occasions. Where they came from was a total mystery. The owner had a number of night-time visitations from what he took to be the ghost of a lady in black, dressed smartly but in the fashion of a much earlier generation. This apparition had a very sorrowful expression, but the owner did not find her appearance threatening so much as puzzling. A neighbour once saw a group of four people in old-fashioned clothes making their way up the front garden path only to vanish before they got to the front door.

The accident was featured in an article in the *Illustrated London News* for January 1875 which contained a drawing of the scene in a local building where

Shipton-on-Cherwell Halt. This simple halt was close to the scene of the accident, but actually on the short branch line to Woodstock. Who said 'bus-stop' halts were only a thing of recent years?

This idyllic scene shows the Oxford Canal close to Shipton-on-Cherwell, the site of the railway accident.

the bodies had been taken for identification purposes. A woman is shown almost prostrate with grief as she picks out her young son as being among the dead. When shown the article, the owner of the house immediately recognised the face of the woman as being that of his nocturnal visitor. The owner reckoned that the burning smell may have been a re-enactment of the fact that the coaches caught fire, while the other phenomena, especially the lady in black, were similar re-enactments of the horrors of that which took place close by in 1874.

The line from Oxford to Banbury opened in 1850 and is still operational.

SHROPSHIRE

Shrewsbury

A local man was crushed to death when part of the station roof collapsed. He returns to the scene periodically, looking as if he's trying to work out exactly what happened.

The magnificent frontage of Shrewsbury Station. The self-confidence which this building displays contrasts sharply with the minimalist qualities of most modern railway buildings.

SOMERSET

Dunster

Dunster is the penultimate station on the lengthy branch line from Taunton to Minehead. In 1862 the West Somerset Railway opened a broad-gauge line from Norton Fitzwarren just to the west of Taunton to Watchet, providing access to what was then an important commercial port. The extension on to Minehead was built by the Minehead Railway and opened in 1874. Both lines were worked at first by the Bristol & Exeter Railway and then by the GWR. A curious anomaly was that while the Minehead Railway was absorbed into the GWR in 1897, the West Somerset retained its independence till 1922. Conversion to standard gauge took place in 1882.

Closure of the line by British Railways in 1971 was perhaps one of the more controversial decisions since the line was still handling considerable passenger traffic, especially in the summer holiday season. It reopened in sections as the West Somerset Railway and now runs through to Bishop's Lydeard as a heritage railway. It is always handy for a preserved railway line to have a ghost — it's good for business — and the West Somerset has one at Dunster. It lurks in the old goods shed and seems to consist of a dark shadow which moves around in the gloomy recesses of the furthest corners of the building in such a manner as to appear very threatening and sinister. It is thought to be the ghost of a railwayman who met with a fatal accident in the shed about seventy years ago.

Stogumber

Sir Francis Drake (*c.*1540–96) is either a swashbuckling heroic mariner or a pitiless pirate, depending largely on whether you come from England or Spain. He was of humble parentage but already a national hero by the time he was wooing Elizabeth Sydenham. However, her aristocratic and snobbish parents looked down on him as being of low birth and forbade the marriage. Drake forlornly went back to sea, consoling himself with more plunder, pillage and perhaps even a spot of rapine. Elizabeth gritted her teeth and prepared for her marriage to a bridegroom chosen by her parents on account of his excellent pedigree. The legend has it that the guests were assembling in Stogumber Church for the ceremony, but as the bridal party were entering the building there was a sudden flash of lightning and a sonorous clap of thunder followed by a huge cannonball falling from the sky and rolling up to the bride's feet. Naturally she took this as evidence that her true love had found out about the imminent marriage and had fired this shot from halfway across the world, as a shot across the bows, expressive of his outrage. Equally naturally, she then defied her parents, frustrated the guests and confounded the would-be bridegroom by refusing to continue with the ceremony. It's easy to guess the rest. Drake, of course, returned, they married and lived happily ever after. A nearby stately home exhibits a meteorite the size of a football which is claimed to have been

Sir Francis Drake in a heroic pose. The Spanish didn't think he was a hero; they thought he was in league with the Devil, or even the Devil himself.

the 'cannonball' which upset the applecart as it were. This story has more than a hint of the apocryphal about it.

Stogumber is an intermediate station on the West Somerset Railway.

Watchet

As far as the authors are aware there are no stories of railway ghosts at Watchet, but there is a harbour which is still used by small commercial craft and through which iron ore mined in the Brendon Hills was despatched in large quantities to South Wales during the Industrial Revolution. It was around the harbour that Samuel Taylor Coleridge (1772–1834) almost certainly met the gnarled old sea dog who provided the inspiration for his extraordinary long poem *The Rime of the Ancient Mariner*. Coleridge spent some years living close by at Nether Stowey. The poem has a powerful nightmare quality about it, and some of it at least is thought to have been written while Coleridge was under the influence of opium, a state with which he became increasingly associated. It is in this work that he gave us the following memorable lines, so apposite for a book concerning ghosts:

Like one, that on a lonesome road
Doth walk in fear and dread,
And having once turned round walks on,
And turns no more his head;
Because he knows, a frightful fiend
Doth close behind him tread.

Watchet Harbour. It is hard to visualise this ever having been a small but busy commercial port.

Statue of the Ancient Mariner. This statue at Watchet was unveiled in 2003 in memory of Coleridge and his poem of the supernatural.

SOUTH YORKSHIRE

Beighton

Beighton is on the eastern extremity of Sheffield and had a station on the northern end of what eventually became the Great Central Railway's line towards Chesterfield, Nottingham, Leicester and London Marylebone. One day back in the 1960s two off-duty railwaymen were walking along the platform of the station, which had been closed in 1954. It was the middle of the day and the two men were chatting about this and that when the hand-lamp one of them was carrying was suddenly pulled out of his grip by an invisible hand and thrown to land some distance away with a crash. Both men were puzzled, and the one who had been holding the lamp was shocked enough by this sudden violence to be quite badly shaken up. He moved to retrieve the lamp, and had only just picked it up when once again it was invisibly snatched away and hurled once more, a bit further this time. Not stopping to recover the lamp on this occasion, they simply legged it away as fast as they could move. They had seen nothing and had no explanation for this strange episode. Was it a ghost with a mean streak? Was there a poltergeist around? Nothing similar has ever been reported from the vicinity.

The line past the old station at Beighton is still operational.

A lady in white clothing looking like that of the Edwardian era has been seen from time to time, but she fades away if approached. Elsecar is served by trains running between Sheffield and Leeds.

Hexthorpe near Doncaster

Hexthorpe lies at the centre of what used to be a complex web of railway lines on the approaches to Doncaster from the south-west. It was on the Sheffield to Doncaster and Grimsby line of the Manchester, Sheffield & Lincolnshire Railway (later the Great Central), and opened in 1849. It was the scene of a horrific accident in 1887. The driver of a MS&L Liverpool to Hull express overran signals and crashed into the rear of a special train to the Doncaster races, which was standing in Hexthorpe ticket platform. Twenty-five people were killed. Ninety-four people were seriously injured.

As so often happens with serious railway accidents, the subsequent inquiry unearthed a farrago of misunderstanding, incompetence, carelessness and out-dated working equipment and practices. First impressions were that the driver and fireman of the Hull express were to blame, and they were arrested and charged with manslaughter. The trial at York Assizes aroused great interest across the nation. It was long-drawn-out, but the jury returned a verdict of 'not guilty'. The MS&L was strongly criticised in the Board of Trade inquiry for slapdash signalling arrangements and for persisting with the use of vacuum brakes rather than automatic continuous brakes on passenger trains.

The response of the company's employees to the accident was in direct con-trast to that of its chairman. The employees offered to forgo a day's wages to help the company defray the costs of the accident. The chairman, Sir Edward Watkin, one of most ruthless and ambitious railway magnates of the nineteenth century, arrogantly argued in favour of the continued use of the vacuum brake despite the fact that the inquiry specifically stated that had the MS&L express been equipped with automatic brakes the accident could have been avoided. With the quite extraordinary effrontery for which Watkin was notorious, he then made a statement expressing his regret that the driver and fireman had been exonerated.

Immediately after the accident the Hexthorpe area gained a reputation for being haunted by ghosts of some of the victims of the disaster, and even by a re-enactment of the crash. There is a theory that the concentration of emotion released by such events can imbue the locality with an energy that leads to such re-enactments. This energy is thought sometimes to dissipate over time, and there have been no reports of such activity for many years.

In the 1970s, however, a number of railway workers reported seeing a mys-terious figure described as a man in a light-coloured raincoat moving about some sidings in the vicinity of Hexthorpe. The apparition sometimes passed uncomfortably close to moving locomotives and wagons, causing worry for the railwaymen, but when they challenged him, he simply vanished. Inevitably those who saw the figure were left wondering if they had been seeing things, but sightings were so persistent that the feeling developed that there was indeed a ghost at Hexthorpe. A few hoaxers and pranksters got in on the act to confuse the issue. A goods guard, however, was left in no doubt that he had seen the

Hexthorpe ghost. He was sitting in his brake-van at the rear of a goods train waiting for clearance from the sidings when a man in a light-coloured raincoat opened the rear door, walked passed him and then vanished through the closed front door of the van.

Was this the ghost of one of the victims of the Hexthorpe crash who had purloined a raincoat to keep himself warm on cold nights, or is there some other explanation for the apparition?

The line from Sheffield to Doncaster is still operational through Hexthorpe.

The Hexthorpe Disaster. As usual, a chapter of misunderstandings, negligence and penny-pinching led to this accident.

SUFFOLK

Bury St Edmunds

The first railway line to Bury St Edmunds was from Ipswich and opened in
1846. In 1854 a connection was completed to Newmarket whence there was
already a line to Cambridge. In 1879 a curve at Chippenham allowed through-
running of trains from Bury to Ely. South from Bury went a rural branch line
to Long Melford, opened in 1865, while northwards was an even more rustic
branch to Thetford, completed in 1876. All these lines eventually came under
the ownership of the Great Eastern Railway and obviously meant that Bury
became a railway junction of some importance.

Bury St Edmunds. This station was opened by the Eastern Union Railway in 1847. It
was a very impressive station for a relatively small town, and once had an overall roof.

As a town and regional centre, Bury was perhaps more important than its mere population figures in the nineteenth century would suggest. The standing in which the railway authorities held Bury is surely indicated by its station. This was opened by the Eastern Union Railway in 1847, replacing a temporary station close by. It probably looked more impressive externally than from the platforms, but it was a grandiose station by any standards. It was built in red brick with stone dressings and the eastern end of the platforms sport a pair of extraordinary Baroque domed towers. It formerly had an overall roof and its façade is an eclectic mix of Tudor with a dash of the Dutch. It is now too large for the traffic it handles, and for much of the time looks somewhat forlorn. Something of a ghost station, perhaps?

Bury Station is a listed structure, as is the adjacent Station Bridge, an underbridge at the east end of the station. This bridge is supposedly haunted. For over 130 years there have been occasional reports of sightings of 'an old-fashioned soldier' in the vicinity. The story goes that this is the ghost of a veteran of the Crimean War who was seriously injured and brought back to be looked after in a hospital in the Bury area. Presumably he made a full recovery because, sound in wind, limb and all the other relevant parts, he met and fell in love with a local nurse. A passionate romance ensued. The father made it known that he disapproved, believing that soldiers had a girl in every port, as it were, and were a bad lot. The couple decided to elope, but her father found out about their plans and he went looking for the soldier. He caught up with him by the railway bridge near Bury Station and shot and killed him.

Trains still run on the Cambridge to Ipswich and the Peterborough and Ely to Ipswich lines.

Felixstowe

Passenger trains first ran to Felixstowe from Westerfield on 1 May 1877, operated by the Felixstowe Railway & Pier Co. of 1875 which was controlled by the local big-shot, Colonel George Tomline. He was the largest landowner in the district and a man of forceful if eccentric personality who wanted to develop Felixstowe as a port to rival nearby Harwich. In 1879 the Great Eastern Railway took over the operation of the line and some trains were extended to and from Ipswich. Tomline's company was then renamed the Felixstowe Dock & Railway Co. and obtained parliamentary authority to build a dock basin. This was not very successful, but, rather unexpectedly and not entirely to Tomline's approval, Felixstowe began to develop into a fashionable seaside watering place. In 1887 the GER bought the railway and in 1898 opened the town station, which was well situated for serving the holiday and residential town that was developing on the cliff top away from the two existing stations called Felixstowe Beach and Pier respectively.

It was on the approach to the town station that many people used to witness what they believed was the ghost of a young girl who had been run over by a train at this point. This spook has not been seen for many years.

This is the rather sad remnant of a well-built four-platform station in Felixstowe, but at least it is still open. The ghostly manifestation is said to have occurred close to the bridge in the distance.

Tomline would be a happy man were he alive today. His port has expanded into a major container depot and base for ferries to Zeebrugge.

Sudbury

In British Railways days the rather pompous term 'motive power depot' was created to replace the more informal 'engine shed'. 'Shed' is most certainly an appropriate word to describe the motive power depot at Sudbury. By any standards the Great Eastern Railway Co. was an impecunious concern with little money to spare for infrastructure, but there are garden sheds that would have put its engine shed at Sudbury to shame.

In 1846 the grandly titled Colchester, Stour Valley, Sudbury & Halstead Railway Co. was incorporated, the main purpose of which was to build a line twelve miles long from the main line of the Eastern Counties Railway at Marks Tey to the prosperous little town of Sudbury. This line opened in 1849. In 1865 it was extended beyond Sudbury to Long Melford where it bifurcated with one branch heading westward to Haverhill and another northward to Bury St Edmunds. These lines were all absorbed by the Great Eastern in 1898.

When this extension was made, a new through station was built and the old terminus was converted into a goods depot. It was on the edge of this goods yard that a small engine shed was erected, perhaps large enough to accommodate two small locomotives under cover. This mean little building was well away from the new station and stood amidst a collection of other shanties which housed the varied freight services provided by the railway for the needs of Sudbury and district. None of these was occupied at night when the branch line closed down, but a man was required to be on duty in the shed and ensure that its locomotives were ready for activity in the morning. This meant that although the man had plenty of work to do on the shift servicing the locomotives, his was a lonely post. He would have been well aware that thieves often found railway sidings and depots a tempting target for their depredations. Contrary to current received wisdom, the 'good old days' never really existed, and even small towns like Sudbury had their criminal fraternities in the nineteenth century, and theft supported by violence was by no means uncommon.

We do not know what went through the mind of the shedman during his nocturnal vigil, but he would only have been human to feel a sense of loneliness and vulnerability. Is it worse to be threatened by a living entity or a dead one, perhaps a ghost? One night in 1923 the man had done all the work that needed doing and was relaxing over a mug of steaming tea in the little room that constituted the office and mess. It was about an hour before any of the drivers or firemen were due to sign in and not too long before his shift would finish. Suddenly, only yards away because the shed was so small, he heard the sound of coal being shovelled from a bunker or tender fall-plate, just as it would sound if a fireman was feeding an engine's firebox. He picked up a lamp and rushed outside, but the moment he did so the sound stopped. He examined both the engines under his care but there was nothing to be seen and so, puzzled, he went back to the office. No sooner had he resumed his seat when the shovelling sound started again. Once more he rushed out – nothing there! Now simply irked rather than puzzled, he had another look round, more thoroughly this time, and then went back to the mess. Three more times the sound reoccurred and then stopped abruptly the minute he opened the door into the shed. After the fifth time the man was a trembling wreck. Gone was any desire to find out what was causing the noise; all he wanted to do was to run away to home and hearth. He knew that if he did he would be dismissed from his post. Fortunately it seemed as if the fifth bout of shovelling had been the last, and he waited patiently, but only partially recovered from the shock, for the first of his colleagues to report in. He resolved to put a brave face on it and not tell any of them of his experience.

It was with a sense of understandable trepidation that he made his way to work the next evening. He knew that he had heard something the previous night. He could have handled the situation had it simply been some stupid prankster. He would have given him a hiding he would never forget. The trouble was that he knew that anyone playing tricks would have given themselves away. He just couldn't reconcile himself to the idea that somebody in Sudbury was stupid enough to walk through the town in the early hours of the morning, trespass on railway property and enter the tiny darkened shed, climb onto a footplate and then simulate the actions of a locomotive fireman, and do so without being discovered. It was too absurd even to contemplate. The problem was that the alternative was worse. Could it have been a ghost? But ghosts were just something you read about in books. Nobody thought they actually existed, or so his rational side argued.

As the last of his colleagues mounted his bike and cycled off into the night, the man realised that he had never felt lonelier. What would he do if the dreaded shovelling started up again? His routine jobs kept him busy for a while. There was some paperwork to do and a few simple pieces of maintenance on the two engines present that night. As usual this work took a couple of hours or more, and he then retired to the mess for a mug of tea poured out from a vast black and somewhat soot-encrusted kettle. Try as he might, he couldn't keep his hand steady as he held the mug and glanced up at the clock. It was almost exactly twenty-four hours since he had heard the mysterious sounds of shovelling. He felt a gnawing in the pit of his stomach as he strained to hear the repetition that he so dreaded. The minutes ticked by in an awful suspense. Five…ten…fifteen. The mess room was hot and the man dozed off. He woke with a jolt – he must have been asleep for an hour. He had a few more chores to do and then he heard a cheerful whistle as the first of his mates arrived for work.

He never heard the sound again nor did he mention it to anyone for years, but then one evening in the pub he and a group of railwaymen were telling yarns. He'd had a pint more than usual and was feeling somewhat garrulous – he only had a few weeks to go before retirement. What he related didn't even raise an eyebrow. Two of the men said that they had heard the same noise but also hadn't mentioned it for fear that they would be thought of as moonstruck. Gossip got around fast in a little town like Sudbury. Another man said that fifty or more years ago a fireman at the shed was the victim of unrequited love and had become so despondent that he had hanged himself nearby. Was it the ghost of this lovelorn man that returned every so often to shovel coal in the witching hours?

The shed was taken down around 1950 – a good shove would probably have done the job – and after that the locomotives stood in the open. Diesels replaced steam and, perhaps surprisingly, the branch line from Marks Tey as far as Sudbury remains operational.

SUSSEX

Balcombe Tunnel

Such was the significance of Brighton in the social and fashionable life of the so-called great and good of Britain that a line between that town and London featured strongly in the list of early railway projects. In fact in 1835 no fewer than six schemes to join them were being considered. In 1837 the London & Brighton Railway received parliamentary authorisation. The first sod was cut on 12 July 1838 and the line opened in September 1841.

The terrain meant this was a heavily engineered line, striking against the grain of the Weald and penetrating the heart of the Downs to reach Brighton. Nowhere is this civil engineering more evident than in the vicinity of Balcombe between Three Bridges and Haywards Heath.

Balcombe Tunnel is 800 yards long, and has long been regarded as haunted. In the first instance it is said that during the First World War three soldiers took shelter in the tunnel during a bombing raid, presumably by a Zeppelin. They may have got away from the bombs but were knocked down and killed by a train instead. Others say that they took shelter during a storm. History repeated itself as tragedy during the Second World War when once again the tunnel was used as a shelter, perhaps during a bombing raid. This time two soldiers entered the tunnel, and they also died courtesy of a fast-moving electric train. So a total of five soldiers breathed their last in Balcombe Tunnel, and there have been many reports that their ghosts have been seen, but as is the way with many ghosts, they simply fade away if any attempt is made to approach them.

Just south of the tunnel is the Balcombe or Ouse Valley Viaduct. This is a claimant for the title of most elegant viaduct in Britain, and its fine lines are evidence of how the early railway builders were successful in combining engineering and art to enhance rather than intrude on the landscape. The viaduct is 492 yards long. It is built of red brick and Caen stone and all the materials were brought to the site by barge up the River Ouse, which was then navigable almost as far as Haywards Heath. The line over the viaduct and through the tunnel is still operational.

Clayton Tunnel

Clayton Tunnel is one mile and 499 yards in length and burrows under the South Downs on the London to Brighton main line of the former London, Brighton & South Coast Railway between Hassocks and Preston Park, just north of Brighton. On Sunday 25 August 1861 it was the scene of an appalling accident, the worst up to that time that had occurred anywhere on Britain's railways. This tunnel is on the same line as that at Balcombe and opened for traffic in 1841.

Early signalling and safety arrangements on the railways strike the modern observer as being rather haphazard or even verging on the slap-happy.

Balcombe Station on the London to Brighton line. This tunnel is just to the north of the station and, close by, to the south, is the magnificent Balcombe or Ouse Viaduct.

The idea of despatching trains on a busy line on the basis of a short time interval seems fraught with obvious dangers. However, there was a justifiable dread of an accident occurring in a tunnel and it was for this reason that the LB&SC had installed a primitive block system worked by electric telegraph in the tunnel. It was the very first such installation on any of Britain's railways. Its inadequacies, other failed equipment and human error were responsible for the horrific crash.

In the enquiry following the accident a farrago of bad practices was unearthed. Not the least of these was that the signalman in Clayton Tunnel south signal box was working a twenty-four-hour shift on that day. This was to allow him to have one full day per week away from work, but it may have accounted for his rather slow responses once things started going wrong; he was simply over-tired. Three trains were scheduled in close succession on the northbound line through the tunnel. They were an excursion from Portsmouth consisting of sixteen coaches, an excursion of seventeen coaches from Brighton and a normal scheduled train of twelve coaches. It was the usual practice on this line for trains to be despatched at intervals of five minutes. The enquiry into what subsequently happened showed that the three trains had actually been booked away from Brighton with three- and-

Clayton Tunnel is odd because it has one plain portal, the other being this extraordinary romantic castellated entrance. The small building peeping coyly over the parapet was originally the tunnel-keeper's cottage.

four-minute intervals between them, although the train register had falsely recorded five and nine minutes respectively.

In simple terms what happened was that the signalman in Clayton Tunnel south box was unable to ascertain from his colleague in the north box at the far end of the tunnel whether the first train had passed through. At the very last minute he showed a red flag to the following train, which was seen by the engine's crew who braked and came to a halt in the tunnel and then, and this seems absolutely extraordinary, began to reverse slowly to check with the signalman what he had meant by flagging them. It was while the second train was backing that it was hit by the third train. On impact, the engine of this train reared up, its chimney hitting the roof of the tunnel, red hot coals going in all directions and scalding steam being released under high pressure. Twenty-three passengers died and 176 others were seriously injured.

The improvement of railway safety has been cumulative and the enquiry into this accident was one of the factors leading to the adoption of block rather than time-interval signalling throughout those parts of Britain's railway system used by passenger trains, and also compulsory continuous brake systems on passenger trains.

Since 1861 there have been sporadic reports from men maintaining the track inside the tunnel of the horrifying sounds of crashing and crunching metal, the release of high-pressure steam and screams of agony. These have been put down to a ghostly re-enactment of the horrors of that dreadful August day in 1861.

Clayton Tunnel is odd because it was built with a plain portal at its southern end and a highly eccentric north end designed to look like a medieval castle gateway. The strange sight this offers is only accentuated by the fact that a little brick cottage peers incongruously and a little self-consciously over the parapet. When it first opened, Clayton Tunnel was lit by gas and it is thought that this cottage may have housed the man who looked after this lighting.

So odd is the effect created by the castle and the cottage that the northern entrance to Clayton Tunnel often features in books on architectural follies and foibles.

West Hoathly

In 1882 the London, Brighton & South Coast Railway opened a line from East Grinstead through Horsted Keynes to Culver Junction where it met the same company's line from Tunbridge Wells, Eridge and Uckfield to Lewes. The new line was a scenic route and gained the nickname of the 'Bluebell Line'. It was also a solidly engineered line built in anticipation of a level of traffic which was never realised. It did not help that several of the stations were a considerable distance from the places they purported to serve. The high hopes for the traffic that would develop were indicated by provision being made for double track on the section south from Horsted Keynes to Culver Junction. The second track was never required although there were passing loops at stations.

In the early 1960s a man was having a quiet holiday pottering around in this delightful part of Sussex. Being interested in railways, he thought he would go and wallow in a bit of pleasant nostalgia tinged with melancholy by visiting the closed 'Bluebell Line', parts of which were in the process of being dismantled. He parked up near West Hoathly Station and decided to have a look at Sharpthorne Tunnel, which was 731 yards in length. It was Saturday afternoon and the demolition contractors had left the site for the weekend. He walked along the formation where the track had been and came up to the tunnel entrance. He was able to see a circle of bright sunlight at the far end. He rather wanted to walk this abandoned tunnel before it was bricked up, and he thought it would only take him about fifteen minutes. He plunged into the darkness eagerly, realising that he was doing something that not many other people would ever do. Some though, he acknowledged, might not have had any wish to do such a thing.

It was surprisingly dark within the tunnel but, although the rails had been ripped up, the ballast was still in place and his feet, which he was unable to see, made a reassuring crunching sound as he stumbled along. Other sounds intruded on his senses. One was the drip-drip of water falling from the tunnel roof in many places; another was his own unnaturally laboured breathing. He realised that this tunnel had 'atmosphere'. He quickly decided that it was an atmosphere that he didn't like, but he pressed on despite increasingly having qualms about the whole venture. It was a bit late to be having second thoughts. The tunnel end he was making for provided a welcoming circle of sunlight, although it didn't seem to be getting any closer. Suddenly a figure was silhouetted against the sunlight. Something a little distance ahead pranced across his line of vision and then disappeared noiselessly. He wasn't quite sure whether it was a human figure – it had moved so swiftly – but on the whole he thought it must have been. He dared not think about what other kind of creature might be lurking in an abandoned railway tunnel.

He stood petrified and rooted to the spot, the steady drip-drip of water and his breathing now being drowned out by another noise: the stentorian beating of his own heart! He had the horrid feeling that whatever he had seen was hiding in wait for him. Perhaps it was eyeing him up at this very moment from one of the little refuges or recesses in the tunnel walls that the platelayers and gangers sheltered in when trains passed. Desperately he looked around him, realising that he was only just about half-way through the tunnel. He was afraid to advance, but the idea of beating a retreat with this thing perhaps dogging his footsteps was equally repugnant. With a superhuman effort he decided to continue but when he tried to put one foot in front of the other, he couldn't move. It was as if he had hit an invisible barrier.

He was scared witless but he made himself turn round and head back the way he had come, albeit looking back nervously over his shoulder every few seconds as he did so. Then he stopped, seeing or sensing nothing untoward. He had had a very bad fright but what had he actually seen? Could it just have been some prankster who at this very moment was chortling away to himself and would undoubtedly be telling his mates down the pub that night how he'd scared away this stupid bloke walking through the old tunnel?

It took much effort on his part but he decided that no local yokel was going to get the better of him in this way, so he reversed direction to head for the far end of the tunnel once more. He had taken no more than a couple of steps when he again experienced the sense of walking into an invisible and immovable barrier. That was too much. He turned round yet again and ran in a blind panic towards the original end of the tunnel. His legs seemed like lead, but this time he dared not look back. What a glorious relief to stumble out into the warmth of a lovely English summer's day full of birdsong.

Covered in a cold sweat, he sat down on a wall to try to regain his composure. The contrast between the reassuring and familiar sights and sounds of the countryside and the sensations in the tunnel could not have been starker. He made a resolution never to walk through an abandoned railway tunnel again. He had had a bad scare and recalling the experience in later years always brought him out in goose pimples. He told a few people about his adventure and learned that the tunnel did have a sinister reputation, local gossip being that it was haunted perhaps by someone who had gone into it for a dare and then been killed by a train. Was it the ghost of this unlucky or just stupid trespasser that the man saw in Sharpthorne Tunnel that day?

Another tunnel on the line, Cinder Hill Tunnel, which is a mere 62 yards long, gained fame in the Second World War when a train used it as a shelter from a German fighter which dived down to strafe it.

The line from East Grinstead to Lewes became notorious in the 1950s. The Acts of 1877 and 1878 which authorised the building of this route specifically stated that a minimum of four trains a day in each direction had to call at Newick & Chailey, Sheffield Park and West Hoathly stations. The line lost money and British Railways Southern Region wanted to withdraw passenger services. The normal procedures were observed and the line was scheduled to lose its passenger services in June 1955, but in the event they ceased earlier due to a national strike by footplatemen. A zealous local resident then informed British Railways that the closure of the three stations was illegal and that the service would have to be restored. This the Southern Region did with extraordinary ill grace. Services were restored running between East Grinstead and Lewes but calling only at these three stations and omitting Barcombe, which was the only one which generated significant traffic! Not only that but the trains ran at the most inconvenient times possible and consisted of some of the most ramshackle coaches in use anywhere in the country. This ridiculous service of what might almost be described as 'ghost trains' ended when British Railways managed to have the original Acts repealed. The locals mockingly called it 'the sulky service'.

In 1908 the London, Brighton & South Coast Railway was reorganising its engineering works at Brighton. Sidings at Horsted Keynes took on the appearance of an elephants' graveyard as an antediluvian selection of the company's locomotives was stored there. Most of them were superannuated engines that would be called in for scrapping once the works resumed its normal activity. There is something extremely ghostly about the sight of the inert, rusting hulks of steam locomotives stored out of use in this way. No wonder that a locomotive not in steam is called a 'dead engine'.

The 'Bluebell Line' in due course became the 'Bluebell Railway', a very successful steam-operated heritage line. It started operations in 1960 and has gone from strength to strength. Work is now (December 2008) well advanced in reopening the northern section to East Grinstead, which means that trains will soon be running once more through Sharpthorne Tunnel. This tunnel is the longest on any of the UK's preserved railway lines.

In the 1960s several hundred steam locomotives gathered in sidings at Barry
Docks awaiting scrapping. Some were there for years, silently rusting away. A 'dead'
locomotive is one not in steam, and there are dead engines as far as the eye can see.
Now do you believe in railway ghosts?

WEST MIDLANDS

Coventry
The first regular trains through Coventry ran on the Rugby to Birmingham
section of the London & Birmingham Railway in 1838. Later on all the lines
that served the city came under the control of the London & North Western
Railway. This company therefore enjoyed a virtual monopoly of Coventry
although they had been forced grudgingly to accept the arch-rival Midland
Railway having running powers over the line from Nuneaton.

The busy Warwick Road runs on a large bridge over the western end of
Coventry Station, and round this area there used to be extensive sidings and
associated goods sheds, offices and other buildings. One of the buildings in
this area had the reputation of being haunted. After being sold out of railway
use, this building found new life as a recording studio, and it was reckoned to
contain not just one but two ghosts. One was the spirit of a railwayman who
has the habit of turning lights on and off unwontedly, and opening and closing
doors and windows, casting a rather frightening shadow of a man's head and
also invisibly brushing past staff and visitors to the studio. There is no actual
evidence of who he was, but his presence in this particular building has led to
the suggestion that he must have been a railwayman. The second ghost is that
of a young man associated with the recording studio who died as the result

Coventry Station looking northwards. The Warwick Road Bridge crosses the end of the station in the distance.

of injudiciously mixing drink and drugs. This ghost was thought to tamper with the sophisticated electrical equipment in the studio with the result that very odd extraneous noises would be heard on some recordings. Between them the two ghosts were able on occasion to produce a distinctly unpleasant atmosphere, and several eminent figures from the world of pop music have commented that they do not like working in the studio because they have felt threatened by a presence or, should we say, two presences.

WEST YORKSHIRE

Clayton

The Midland, the Lancashire & Yorkshire and the Great Northern railway companies were deadly rivals in parts of the West Riding of Yorkshire, never more so than in the area to the west of Bradford towards Halifax and Keighley. When one company sought parliamentary approval for a line, one or other of its rivals would immediately set about planning a line of their own in the vicinity. This meant, for example, that there were two rival routes between Bradford and Halifax and Bradford and Keighley, admittedly serving different intermediate places.

The Great Northern did not have the pick of the routes joining Bradford to these other important towns because the Lancashire & Yorkshire already had a route via Low Moor to Halifax and the Midland had a line to Keighley via Shipley and Bingley. The very high ground to the west of Bradford around Queensbury (over 1,100ft above sea level) did not attract much in the way of interest from early railway promoters until the Bradford & Thornton Railway Co. was incorporated in 1871 and absorbed by the Great Northern in the following year. A line had already been built from Halifax to Ovenden and the Great Northern decided to extend this line to Queensbury to connect with the line from Bradford. At the same time as thereby gaining access to Halifax, the Great Northern announced its intention of building a line from Queensbury to Keighley. The lines concerned opened in sections between 1878 and 1884, quite late in the day for new railway construction.

These schemes had as much to do with railway imperialism as they did with serious commercial considerations. To this day much of the territory which these lines penetrated remains predominantly rural. The lines which converged on Queensbury were immensely expensive to construct, with several tunnels, numerous massive viaducts and such fearsome gradients that the Great Northern footplatemen called this part of the line from Bradford to Holmfield 'the Alpine Route'. No expense was spared in the building of these lines, and yet there was little hope of generating much intermediate business. At the more urbanised Bradford and Halifax ends of the lines, the introduction of electric trams soon leached away much of the local traffic. The Queensbury lines cost almost £1 million to build and can never have repaid the initial investment. Normal passenger services were withdrawn in 1955 and the lines west of Horton Park were closed completely by 1965, with a stub surviving for freight purposes at the eastern end of the line until 1972.

In the late 1940s a young man who lived in Clayton used to catch the train to Great Horton where he worked in a mill. One freezing cold and clear moonlit night he stood on the platform at Great Horton after work waiting for the local train to take him back to Clayton and his dinner and a roaring fire. The train heaved itself up the gradient into the station, dead on time. As usual it was hauled by one of the sturdy little Ivatt 0-6-2 tank engines and consisted, as always, of two rather ancient compartment carriages. He chose an empty compartment and climbed in to the reassuringly familiar dusty and well-worn surroundings made comparatively cosy with their steam-heating. At least it was a lot warmer than standing on the platform.

With a pop in its whistle, the engine set off climbing hard to Clayton, the next station along the line. As the train entered a deep cutting, the hitherto warm and welcoming compartment suddenly became freezing cold and, to his horror, the young man looked up to see a woman's face pressed against the outside of the window. And what a face! It was twisted into a grimace of pain and terror which itself managed to be utterly terrifying. He sank back into his seat, his own face a mask of shock and fear. Thankfully the face at the window vanished just before the train staggered into Clayton Station. Shaking like an aspen, the young man leapt out of the compartment and almost fell into the arms of a porter on the platform. As a regular traveller, he was on first name terms with the man.

There was something comforting both in the solid feel of the station buildings and in the solid appearance and demeanour of the porter to whom the frightened young man gasped out his story. The porter calmed him down and told him that he had seen the ghost of 'Fair Becca'. It transpired that the young man was only the latest of many travellers on the line who in the hours of darkness had had a similar experience. Becca was a married woman who, many years previously, had enjoyed an extra-marital affair which her husband had found out about. Having an insanely jealous nature, he was not the sort to sit down and talk it through. He told her he was going to kill her, and that's precisely what he did. Left with the perennial problem of all murderers, that of disposing of the body, he didn't use much thought and simply dumped it down a well where it was only a matter of time before it was discovered. Fair Becca's ghost haunted the stretch of line between Great Horton and Clayton, close to the place where she was murdered.

Haworth

Haworth, famous for its associations with the extraordinary literary Bronte sisters, and Branwell, their boozy brother, was a station on the branch line from Keighley to Oxenhope. This line climbed steeply from the northern terminus at Keighley following the River Worth, and the company under whose auspices it was built was not unnaturally called the Keighley & Worth Valley Railway It opened in 1867 and was taken over by the giant Midland Railway in 1881. That company had operated the trains right from the start.

In fact the line had an inauspicious history even before it opened. A cow is said to have eaten the engineering plans related to the line. Presumably they were the only copy because the start of construction work was delayed. The building of the short Ingrow Tunnel undermined a newly built Methodist chapel which collapsed leaving the railway company having to pay compensation. Shortly before the line was due to open great storms caused the Worth to go into spate and wash away a bridge near Damems. On the rearranged day for the line's opening, the inaugural train had to have two goes at climbing the 1 in 58 out of Keighley. It was completely defeated by the gradient between Oakworth and Haworth and the only option was to split the train in two. Happily both portions managed to make it to Oxenhope, but a legend of unintentional and understated comedy had already been created which the line found it easy to live up to.

The old goods yard at Haworth houses much of the rolling stock and equipment for the preserved Worth Valley Railway, and the vicinity has gained the reputation of being haunted by the ghost of a man with the strange name of Binns Bancroft. He was a coal merchant who ran his business from the railway yard at Haworth in the late nineteenth century. He seems to have been a busybody because he insisted on supervising the shunting operations when the pick-up goods train arrived to drop off wagons of coal for him. Despite not being a railway employee he often actually undertook the quite hazardous job of using a shunting pole to unhook moving wagons, and he dashed about the sidings issuing instructions to the men on the engine and to the guard. They regarded him as a perishing nuisance. His zeal eventually got the better of him and he died after being crushed between two wagons. This was in 1882. The verdict at his inquest was 'death by misadventure'.

Some people reckon that Binns Bancroft's body may have been buried but his soul goes marching on. The figure of a man has been seen in and around the yard, sometimes with a shunting pole in his hand and gesticulating as if he was perhaps directing shunting operations. Many people claim to have seen a figure answering this description, but any attempts to approach him merely cause him to fade away. Items have been moved around in the yard at times when the public have been excluded and when none of the volunteers have been around. They have sometimes been hidden away and it has been the Devil's own work to find them again. It seems that Binns Bancroft is as capable of being a nuisance dead as when he was alive.

As with so many branch lines, the Keighley & Worth Valley enjoyed its best years in the 1930s. Cuts were made in services during the Second World War and again in the 1950s, but an enhanced service operated by diesel multiple units was introduced in 1960, by which time closure of the line had already been threatened. Earlier economies had included the use of a three-coach gangwayed set of carriages which enabled the guard to issue tickets on the train. The regular guard was a man of splenetic and misanthropic character whose ticket machine enabled him to issue tickets for a range of destinations beyond the branch line itself, but for reasons of his own he preferred not to do so. On one occasion a woman passenger asked him for a return to Bingley, not very far away on the line between Keighley and Leeds. He grumbled that he did not know the fare and would have to return to the guard's van to consult his faretable. She stuck to her guns, he went off and returned audibly griping about the inconvenience to which he was being put. The ticket was sold and money changed hands but he told her next time she wanted to do the trip to Bingley and back, she should go by bus.

Passenger services were withdrawn in 1961 and freight followed within a few years. However, the Keighley & Worth Valley Railway Preservation Society had been established and they bought the line, restoring services and its Victorian atmosphere, and creating a successful tourist attraction.

Damems is a stopping place on what is now known as the Worth Valley Railway. It has a short platform and the station building was so small that local legend said that a nearby farmer once requisitioned it for use as a hen hut. Damems was widely regarded as the smallest station in the mighty and widespread empire operated by the Midland Railway. A ghostlike figure wearing the uniform of a railwayman has been seen in the vicinity on a number of occasions.

The Worth Valley Railway is quite a place for the aficionado of the supernatural. One of the features of the line which juvenile passengers in particular love is Ingrow Tunnel. How is one to explain the sight of smoke, having the appearance and smell of that produced by a steam locomotive, pouring out of the entrance of the tunnel? This phenomenon would be entirely understandable if a steam-hauled train had just passed through but makes absolutely no sense when it occurs on days when none of the locomotives are steam-driven.

Huddersfield

Huddersfield is a product of the Industrial Revolution and its early prominence in the use of steam power in the woollen industry meant that a canal was built linking the Calder-Hebble navigation to Lancashire through the heart of the Pennines. Traffic began in 1811, but the Huddersfield Narrow Canal suffered because the nature of the terrain it passed through which limited its size. By the 1820s there were calls to build a railway to replace it. However, in the speculative binge that established so many railways in the 1830s, Huddersfield missed out and the town was not really on the railway map until 1847. However, the station which was eventually built was an absolute tour de force. It was described by Sir John Betjeman as 'the most splendid station façade in England', and he went on to liken it to an enormous classical country house. It became an important centre of operations for the Lancashire & Yorkshire and London & North Western railway companies. It is still busy.

This station, which is better outside than in, was haunted by the ghost of a man who worked there as a platform porter. Unfortunately he was hit by a train and received injuries which meant that he was incapacitated and had to leave the railway service. It was reckoned that he had been negligent and so he was due no compensation. When he died, probably in the direst of poverty, he apparently returned to his former workplace. For many years when anything went wrong on the premises – a derailment, a minor bump between trains or even parcels falling onto the track and being squashed under a passing train – then a vindictive, gloating laugh would be heard reverberating around under the station's overall roof.

Otley

There are no trains today at Otley. The station opened on 1 February 1865 and closed on 20 March 1965. It was on the former Midland Railway and had been served over the years by trains between Leeds, Ilkley and Skipton, and others from Bradford to Harrogate.

A few miles to the east of Otley ran the Leeds Northern Railway which connected Leeds with Harrogate, Ripon and the north-east of England. This line was opened from Leeds to Thirsk in 1849 and eventually came under the control of the North Eastern Railway Co. The terrain between Leeds and Harrogate is extremely hilly and provided many challenges for the engineers. At Bramhope they had no option but to build a long tunnel, two miles and 241 yards long, to be exact, piercing the watershed between Airedale and Wharfdale. 2,300 men and 400 horses were employed on the works which took four years to be completed. Severe difficulties included constant flooding, and the pumps had to remove no less than 1,600 million gallons of water. There was a human cost to all this. Twenty-three men lost their lives in the building of Bramhope Tunnel and countless others received serious injuries.

In the churchyard of All Saints at Otley is a remarkable monument. It was paid for by the contractor, the sub-contractors and the navvies who chipped in with a whip-round. It takes the form of a replica of the northern entrance to Bramhope Tunnel. The full-size tunnel entrance is remarkable enough, consisting of two mock-Gothic towers complete with arrow slits and battlements, and these are reproduced faithfully at both ends of the replica which stands about 6ft high with a short stretch of tunnel in between. Curiously it does not mention how many navvies were killed or the names of any of them, but it does mention the contractor James Bray and displays a number of biblical quotations. A cynic might conclude that it is more a monument to Bray than to the men who died doing his work. They are buried close by and for many years it was rumoured that this fenced-off bit of churchyard was haunted by their ghosts. Unfortunately, the authors have been unable to discover whether these ghosts themselves were scaled down versions of the prototype. Big or small, the ghosts were real enough to the local schoolchildren who would run past the churchyard as fast as their legs would carry them, not daring to glance towards the monument.

There was something of a craze for adorning railway tunnel mouths with features loosely derived from medieval military architecture. Many early travellers were nervous about their trains plunging into these subterranean passages. Doom and gloom merchants prophesied that tunnel roofs would collapse onto passing trains with all the passengers being crushed to death. Giving the tunnel entrance motifs from centuries-old buildings was no mere whimsy but was done to suggest permanence and thereby to allay the fears of timid passengers.

The line through Bramhope Tunnel is still operational.

Wakefield Kirkgate

The railway history of the Wakefield area is extremely complicated so suffice it to say that, of the city's two stations, this one was under the joint ownership of the Lancashire & Yorkshire and the Great Northern railway companies. It opened for business in 1857.

The memorial in Otley to the victims of the building of Bramhope Tunnel.

The Navvies' Memorial. Local children used to dare each other to crawl through – the ghosts of the navvies might get them!

Even the frontage of Wakefield Kirkgate Station is hardly an advert for rail travel.

Kirkgate Station, in our opinion, is an absolute disgrace. It was once an impressive and busy station with an overall roof. Many passenger trains were to be seen, there were extensive carriage and goods sidings and a real sense of bustle. Now the place is a largely empty, echoing, run-down husk which gives all the wrong impressions about travelling by rail in the twenty-first century. Such is its state of neglect that it might almost be described as a 'ghost station'. It is certainly not the kind of place anyone would want to hang about in, and it is therefore somewhat surprising that it has a ghost who has been seen on many occasions. She takes the form of a lady in clothes of the Victorian period and, although she has been seen in various parts of the station, she seems to prefer to lurk in the dingy subway. Perhaps she is waiting for better times. It may be a long wait.

Yeadon

Yeadon is best known today for being the location of the airport serving Leeds and Bradford, but for some years it was the terminus of a now largely forgotten railway, just one and a half miles long. In the 1880s a proposal was made for a branch from Guiseley on the Leeds and Bradford to the Ilkley line of the Midland Railway to Yeadon. The company making this proposal was the Guiseley, Yeadon & Rawdon Railway, and it got delusions of grandeur that it would extend beyond Yeadon to serve other places in the West Riding. These hopes came to nothing and the short branch was taken over by the Midland

Railway and opened in 1894. This curious little line never had a regular passenger service, was closed temporarily in 1944 as a wartime economy, reopened and then closed permanently in 1964.

Very occasional excursion trains ran on the Yeadon branch, and it was one of these that constituted a ghost train of sorts. The year was 1930 and the LMSR had offered a day excursion from Yeadon to Morecambe. The draw of Morecambe proved irresistible (how could it have been otherwise?) and the train was fully booked. A large crowd of well-wishers turned out to see the train off early in the morning on its scenic route via Ilkley, Skipton, Hellifield and Carnforth. A big crowd of friends, relations and others turned out eager to witness its return. After all, a passenger train at Yeadon was a rare event. The time for its arrival came and went. No one thought anything of a delay of ten minutes or perhaps half-an-hour but when an hour had passed people began to become restless and irritated. After ninety minutes a degree of concern began to spread, but people were helpless because no members of the railway staff were on hand at Yeadon. Rumours began to spread with the quite remarkable speed they often display in such situations. As always, those who knew least said most. Soon theories were circulating that there had been a derailment, a crash or some other catastrophe, and the more suggestive in the crowd began to fear for their kith and kin.

The cause of the problem was an oversight on the part of the LMSR. The line to Yeadon was heavily graded and a pilot engine was required to assist the train engine up to the terminus. They had forgotten to provide a pilot and the train had stopped at Guiseley while attempts were made to rustle up an additional engine from somewhere. These efforts were fruitless and so the harassed staff at Guiseley had little option but to ask everyone on board to alight and to walk the lanes and field paths back to home and hearth. Naturally many passengers were outraged and let their feelings be known. There were many babies on the train and they were getting fractious, as were the children who were now dog-tired after a day of excitement. As usual, the managers whose incompetence was responsible for the failure to provide the pilot engine were many miles away and it was the ordinary railway workers at Guiseley who had to bear the brunt of the justifiable wrath of the frustrated excursionists. However, in dribs and drabs they set off for Yeadon on foot, grumbling as they went and swearing that they would never have anything to do with the railway in the future.

Not surprisingly, the Morecambe excursion became known locally as the 'Ghost Train' – the train that went but never came back.

WILTSHIRE

Box Tunnel
Box Tunnel was perhaps the major engineering feature on the London to Bristol route of what became the Great Western Railway. It is one of Britain's

most impressive railway tunnels and was the work of the immortal Isambard Kingdom Brunel (1806–59). If ever there was a man with a sense of theatre, it was Brunel. Here he built a tunnel which, with its classical portals, was designed to show how engineering and art could be combined in making a dramatic addition to the landscape. It is 3,212 yards long and built on a descending gradient of 1 in 100 going westwards towards Bath and Bristol. Those whose sole purpose in life seems to have been the forecasting of doom and gloom said that if the brakes failed on a train entering the eastern end, it would emerge from the western, that is, the lower end, at a speed of 120 mph, a velocity which would suffocate all the passengers. Others with equally avid relish argued that that such a long tunnel would inevitably collapse and crush a train passing through with a horrible death for all those on board. Fortunately neither of these melodramatic scenarios actually occurred.

However, the building of the tunnel was a project of heroic proportions. The tunnel had to be bored through solid rock, and so daunting a prospect was this that it was difficult to find contractors prepared to take the job on. The rock had to be broken with gunpowder before the miners could tackle it with picks. It was hot, damp, dark and unventilated; a nightmare scene. The workings were constantly flooded and quicksands were encountered. The spoil had to be winched up the construction shafts to the surface and the men got to their place of work by being winched down the shafts in baskets. It is hardly surprising that over 100 men lost their lives during the five years it took to build the tunnel. It opened without ceremony on 30 June 1841.

With so much drama and tragedy accompanying the building of the tunnel, it is hardly surprising that Box has attracted tales of the supernatural. Right from the start, the drivers of locomotives passing through the tunnel claim to have seen figures on the track, often silhouetted against the light at the tunnel mouth. Maintenance men whose job it is to walk the tunnel also report seeing spectral presences and some have gone so far as to describe them as looking like nineteenth-century labourers. The sound of steam-hauled trains passing through the tunnel long after regular steam ended on the Western Region of British Railways has been heard on many occasions. Equally puzzling is the sound of trains passing through the tunnel at times when it has been closed to all traffic for maintenance purposes.

A persistent legend attached to Box Tunnel is that Brunel designed the tunnel so that an observer standing at its western entrance on 9 April, his birthday, and looking through the straight bore, would be able to see the sun rising in the east and casting its rays through the entire length of the tunnel. This has always been taken as evidence of Brunel's engineering genius and sense of the dramatic. Unfortunately, it is not true.

By way of a footnote, Great Western Railway signal boxes sported a rather attractive cast-iron plate on the front of the building which told the world the signal box's name. That at the nearby Box Station was succinct and sym-

The western portal of Box Tunnel, designed in elegant style by I.K. Brunel. The tracks here were originally broad gauge.

metrical. It simply said 'Box Signal Box'. The line through the tunnel is still operational.

Monkton Farleigh Mine

A short distance south-west of Box, under the hill on which the stumpy little curiosity known as 'Brown's Folly' stands, lies what for decades was one of Britain's best-kept secrets. Those who knew of its existence were required by the Official Secrets Act not to reveal this information to anyone. It was virtually an underground city. It covered 80 acres and was possibly the largest underground ammunition dump in the world!

This mysterious place was located in the long defunct Monkton Farleigh stone mine. The labyrinth of caves under the hill was identified by the Government in the 1930s as having the potential for use in wartime as a storage point for ammunition and/or other war supplies. A decision was reached to utilise the existing warren of caves and to create large extensions to the complex which would allow the storage of huge quantities of potentially volatile

Some people believe that the ghost of Brunel returns to this example of his
engineering genius, Box Tunnel.

material deep below ground where the temperature and humidity would be more-or-less constant. The place provided the ideal conditions for an ammunition dump. A great advantage was that the proposed site in the erstwhile mine stood close to the main line from Swindon to Bath and Bristol, owned by the then Great Western Railway, and so the necessarily heavy, awkward and dangerous materials could be transported in and out by rail. Exchange sidings were built connecting it with a narrow-gauge railway system penetrating into the hillside.

A hugely expensive building project was put into effect, costing billions of pounds by today's standards. The complex even had its own medical centre and power station. It is estimated that 7,500 men were employed on the construction works, but only comparatively small numbers of men at any one particular time so that none of them were able to gain an overall view of what the entire project involved. Secrecy and security were maintained at the highest possible level while the work was going on and even more so once hostilities had commenced. A large workforce was in place during the war consisting largely of forces personnel but also considerable numbers of civilians, and again security requirements saw to it that each worker on the site was restricted just to his or her department and not permitted to enter other parts of the establishment. Patrols and pillboxes made it inadvisable for strangers, innocent or otherwise, to get too close.

Every effort was made to try to ensure the maximum possible safety on the site. All sorts of rumours circulated in the surrounding towns and villages about what exactly was going on at Monkton Farleigh and inevitably, once the Second World War started, it became widely but unofficially known that explosives were stored there. The locals might well have had reason to protest had they known that at the peak there were over 12 million shells being stored. A major explosion would have taken Box, Bathford and much of Bath itself with it.

In the late 1970s a museum was created in the then long disused underground complex, but somehow it did not seem to catch on and it closed within a few years. All is peaceful in the Monkton Farleigh area now but traces of the former activities can be found by the determined rambler around OS grid reference 800675. No ghosts have been reported associated with the mine but there is something undeniably eerie about this onetime hive of sinister activity and of any remaining relics associated with it. Also eerie is the idea of 'ghost trains' despatched from elsewhere to this destination 'somewhere in southern England' and which it was an offence to photograph let alone ask about. Despatching trains across Britain required locomotives, train-crew and rolling stock being provided for them, timetable paths being created, even wagon labels being written up and the progress of the train being carefully monitored from signal box to signal box as it proceeded on its way. The operation of these trains must have been an open secret, yet their existence was officially denied.

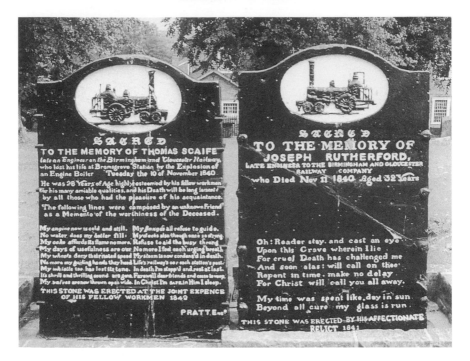

Headstones in Bromsgrove churchyard remembering those employed by the Birmingham & Gloucester Railway who were killed when the boiler of their locomotive exploded in November 1840. The ghosts of Driver Rutherford and Fireman Scaife are thought to rise from their graves from time to time.

Ghost trains, indeed, which ran to officially secret sidings where their contents was transhipped into equally secret narrow-gauge wagons and moved into a place that didn't exist.

WALES

Saltney Ferry

Saltney Ferry (Mold Junction) Station served passenger trains on the line from Chester to Mold and Denbigh. About three and a half miles west of Chester, it stood next to a motive power depot, which was a posh name for a place where locomotives were housed – in other words, an 'engine shed'. This shed went by the name of Mold Junction and the platform at Saltney Ferry provided a good place for trainspotters to take the numbers of the locomotives housed there or just visiting. The Saltney district became an important one, from the railway point of view, with the engine shed, two stations, engineering workshops, a branch line down to wharves on the River Dee and two marshalling yards.

Railways, until the run-down of freight and mineral traffic and the modernisation from the 1960s, were highly labour intensive and a substantial amount of property in the Saltney district was given over to housing railway workers and their families.

The area around Saltney Ferry Station was said to have been haunted by the ghost of an old man seen – but more often heard – pedalling around the area on a rusty bicycle with a notable squeak and a spookily flickering lamp. He did this during the witching hours of early morning darkness, and was spotted over the years by a number of railwaymen going to and from work on shifts involving anti-social hours. It was thought that he was the ghost of a man who had hanged himself in one of the railway buildings at Saltney.

Saltney Ferry Station closed in 1962 when passenger services were withdrawn between Chester and Denbigh. Mold Junction shed closed in 1966 and the marshalling yards were also run down and finally closed. There is little to tell the visitor of the past importance of Saltney in the history of the railways of Chester and North Wales. However, on the opposite side of the Crewe to Holyhead main line, which is still operational, stands a rather gaunt building which was a hostel for railway workers and which has now been converted into flats.

More surprisingly, Mold Junction engine shed survives. It is semi-derelict but houses part of a scrap yard. For those who have fond memories of engine sheds, it is still instantly recognisable for what it was, despite over forty years having passed since the sad occasion on which the last steam locomotive clanked away for work elsewhere or to meet its fate, cut up as so many of them were and the metal of which they were composed reprocessed for use as razor blades.

Mold Junction shed is indeed a place of ghosts.

Talybont-on-Usk

Brecon was a small but important town situated on the River Usk in which by the 1840s the business community felt was being held back by not being located on a railway. Local landowners and commercial interests therefore decided to sponsor a line south to Dowlais and Merthyr from where access would be possible to the whole of industrial and mining South Wales and particularly Newport, forty-seven miles away. The Brecon & Merthyr Tydfil Railway opened in 1863 from Brecon to Pant, and finally to Dowlais in 1869. It was a line with fearsome gradients as it drove southwards through the heart of the Brecon Beacons. Over six miles were on a gradient of 1 in 38 to a summit at Torpantau of 1,313ft above sea level. Coming northwards, Torpantau was reached via a gruelling climb at 1 in 47.

Talybont-on-Usk was a wayside station about seven miles south of Brecon. The line closed in 1962 and the station was eventually converted into an Outdoor Adventure Centre. The story goes that a party of schoolchildren were asleep one night in a dormitory when they were suddenly woken up by the sound of a steam train followed by crashing noises and screams. It was only in the morning that the children who all thought it had been a lark found out that there had been a railway accident at Talybont many years earlier and that perhaps the noise they heard was a ghostly reconstruction. There was indeed a fatal accident in 1878 and this had led to the development of a legend of a ghost train passing along the formation of the old railway, usually around ten past nine when the accident occurred.

SCOTLAND

Auldearn

Auldearn is a small village which possesses a very fine seventeenth-century dovecote, or doocot as they call them in these parts. Three miles east is the Hardmuir, a stretch of woodland which is thought to be the scene for the encounter of Macbeth and Banquo with the witches.

It is therefore entirely appropriate that Auldearn was the scene for the most remarkable of all Scottish witchcraft trials. This took place in 1662. Even without being tortured, the victim, a young girl, confessed to taking part in a series of bizarre rites. At her trial she confirmed most of the popular beliefs about witches – that their meetings were in covens numbering thirteen, they attended baptisms at which the Devil officiated and enjoyed satanic orgies in the woods. She admitted that she and her companions mounted straws, recited a spell and then rode around on the straws, transforming themselves at will into cats, hares and jackdaws. She went on to describe in lurid detail how the Auldearn coven had murdered the children of a local landowner. She related with gory relish how they had made clay effigies of the children and then thrust these into a fire thereby causing the children to die slow and extremely painful deaths. She also admitted to being on intimate terms with the Devil himself. She seems happily to have put herself in the frame for being a witch and a murderer, but there is no historical record of her fate. It is unlikely that she was presented with the freedom of Auldearn and more likely that she was burnt at the stake.

Auldearn formerly had a wayside station on what became the Highland Railway's part of the Inverness to Aberdeen line. It closed in 1960.

Dunphail to Dava

In the 1840s complicated networks of railway lines were opening up in the heavily populated and industrialised Scottish Lowlands with their abundant coal and other mineral resources. Naturally the railway companies involved invested enthusiastically in this part of Scotland, licking their lips at the prospect of the lucrative returns from the business that was likely to be generated in that region. They were not so eager to turn their attention to the building of lines in the much more sparsely populated and less promising areas north and west of Perth. This left the citizens of Inverness and various other northern Scottish towns nursing a strong sense of grievance. It was already evident that railways were powerful generators of industrial and commercial activity and that those places that were left off the railway map or poorly served by railways were likely to stagnate and suffer from literally being off the beaten track.

This issue rumbled on for years without anything very positive happening. The Highlanders advanced the argument that much of northern Scotland had been opened up as a result of the roads built by General Wade in the eighteenth century. These roads had been largely paid for by the Government and, despite being designed primarily for military purposes, they had brought many economic benefits to impoverished parts of Scotland. Wasn't it therefore time for the Government to reinvigorate the area by providing incentives for railway development in the region? Appeals for Government largesse fell on deaf ears, however. In the late 1840s local businessmen in Inverness began to consider the building of a railway to Aberdeen as far as possible along the south shore of the Moray Firth through Nairn, Forres and Elgin and then southwards using a number of river valleys to Aberdeen. This, at the time, seemed like the only feasible route to Aberdeen, the Lowlands and England. It was a roundabout route, but better than nothing. Some of the Aberdonian business community in turn were considering a railway from their city towards Inverness, using much the same route.

Inverness people would have preferred a route southwards towards Perth and the Lowlands, but the terrain between the two places seemed insurmountable given the power of steam locomotives at the time. In the event the Inverness party went ahead with obtaining parliamentary approval for a line eastwards to Nairn being built in the hope of benefiting the two linked towns, but apparently also as being seen as the possible first leg of a route to Perth. The Nairn line opened for passengers in November 1855, isolated from any other railway lines. In 1858 the Nairn line was extended eastwards to meet the Great North of Scotland line from Aberdeen at Keith.

The Nairn line had a very beneficial impact on the economies of Inverness and Nairn and it was not long before the idea of the Perth route resurfaced. Such a line, it was believed, would even more effectively put Inverness 'on the map'. The Inverness & Perth Junction Railway was set up in a heady wave of enthusiasm not least because technology had moved on rapidly and locomotives could now be designed to scale the lofty summits required of a line south to Perth. The first sod was cut in October 1861 for a line south from Forres to Dunphail, across Dava Moor to Aviemore and on to Kingussie, Blair Athol and Perth. Crossing Dava Moor involved gradients of 1 in 70, and the exposed moors in the vicinity were particularly susceptible to heavy snow. This particular part of the route opened in 1864 and later became part of the financially challenged Highland Railway.

It was on the Forres to Aviemore section of what had by then become part of the Highland Railway that a mysterious event occurred in October

1919. A man who lived at the hamlet of Achanlochen had been spending the evening with a friend at Berryburn, and it was approaching midnight on a brightly moonlit night when he left to cycle home, intending to make some use of a track that ran along the side of the railway. When he got there, suddenly in front of him was a light so brilliant that he was forced to look away. Confused and not a little frightened, he got off his bicycle to attempt to investigate the phenomenon only to find it gradually fading away before he was any the wiser about what had caused it. As he made his way home, he was totally perplexed and must have wondered whether he had been hallucinating. He slept fitfully and resolved first thing the next morning to return to the railway and find out whether anyone else had seen the light. Here he was in luck because the first railwayman he met had also been out the previous night and seen the same mysterious bright light. He reported that a number of other people had also seen it. No one could provide any rational explanation and the general consensus was that something supernatural was at the bottom of the mystery. Whatever it was, there were no reports before nor have there been any since.

It may be churlish to mention it, but opinions on the reliability of the witness may be influenced by the fact that about two years earlier he claimed to have seen a cattle train on fire in the sky! Being charitable, we could say that this was associated with a previous accident on the line in which a cattle train had caught fire and the unfortunate creatures had all been immolated. Could it be that the powerful spirit associated with this part of Scotland had some influence on what he saw or thought he saw? After all, there are several distilleries close by.

The line across Dava Moor closed in 1965. The southern end of the line has reopened as the Strathspey Railway.

Kyle of Lochalsh

The fabled line from Dingwall to Kyke of Lochalsh was built by the Dingwall & Skye Railway Co. and was intended in the first instance to provide a boost for the livestock farmers of the districts through which it passed, enabling them to deliver their animals to the markets quickly by rail and in far better condition than if they had been herded on the hoof for hundreds of miles. It was also intended to help the fishing communities of what was then part of Ross & Cromarty to despatch their highly perishable catches far more quickly to markets in the more highly populated parts of Scotland.

The Highland Railway took the line over in 1877. Until 1897 the 'Road to the Isles' terminated at Strome Ferry but an extension to Kyle of Lochalsh opened in that year. Protestant fundamentalism was rife in these parts and not all of the meagre local population welcomed the development of railways. Sabbatarianism was deeply entrenched in these parts and led to many problems at Strome Ferry after the line opened and the railways tried to move wagons containing fish on a Sunday, this being generally held as a day on which no work for gain should under any circumstances be carried out. Obviously fish was a highly perishable cargo which the company needed to move as quickly as possible. No Sunday trains normally ran on the line, so attempting to run a special train on a Sunday in 1883 evoked ferocious and self-righteous wrath from the locals. A group of fishery workers refused to load a consignment of herrings and a fight broke out when the managers of the fishing company tried to load the fish. The Highland Railway was an impecunious company and it needed all the revenue it could get, and so it appealed to the Home Secretary. He despatched a force of burly Edinburgh police officers to ensure that the law was observed and tempers were allowed to cool. This did the trick. The sequel to this incident occurred when the Highland Railway billed the constabulary for the train fares of the officers who had travelled to Strome Ferry. The company graciously gave a discount on the fares but that made no difference to the Commissioner of Police who flatly refused to pay, failing to see why his force should pay the Highland for the privilege of protecting the company's own property.

While Sabbatarianism provoked this militancy, many of the local population had their misgivings about the coming of the railways per se, largely because they were seen as 'unnatural' and also because they would open up this hitherto remote part of Scotland to all the malign, godless influences of modern civilisation. The Highland folk were great believers in omens and, shortly before the extension to Kyle of Lochalsh was completed, many of them claim to have seen a spectral steam-hauled train rushing balefully along the road leading to the Kyle. This apparition manifested itself only at night, but the locomotive made a fearful sight because it belched fire and brimstone and was equipped with piercing headlights. It cavorted down the narrow road and then eventually veered off across the nearby hills and lochs. Obviously no good could come of such an omen.

As a footnote to the issue of Sabbatarianism, it is worth recording that after the Tay Bridge Disaster, several clergymen used the event as the subject for their sermons and dwelt with undisguised relish on the fate of those who had so heinously chosen to travel by train on a Sunday.

The Glasgow Subway

Glaswegians have a great affection for the underground railway that serves their city, or at least some parts of it. They call it the 'Clockwork Orange', or the 'Subway', refusing to kow-tow to the city fathers who would prefer to dignify it with the name 'Underground'. The route is about six and a half miles in length, not circular in shape, and it serves fifteen stations. It opened to the public on 14 December 1896.

It may be a small system but in proportion to its length it has done quite well for attracting mysterious events. The best-known of these is the story of the so-called 'Grey Lady' whose ghost has reportedly been seen in the tunnels around Shields Road Station in what is now a very lonely and depopulated part of the 'Southside'. In 1922 a woman and a small girl inexplicably fell off an almost empty platform onto the track. A station worker leapt to their rescue. His gallant effort saved the girl but the woman died. Her spirit has seemingly refused to leave the scene.

One night the trains had stopped running and were being marshalled for maintenance purposes at the Govan depot. One of the tasks of the workers on the night shift was to check that no passengers were actually left on board – those who perhaps had fallen asleep, for example. On this occasion a team of five men passed through a number of carriages and, sure enough, there was a man apparently happily dozing, dressed in a raincoat and wearing a flat cap like so many thousands of others in the city. They woke him up and told him that he had to follow them through the empty rolling stock and out to the street entrance. He seemed perfectly amenable although rather slow on his feet, and he followed them as instructed. They repeatedly looked back to allow him to catch up and they had just got to the exit from the depot when they looked back for the final time only to find that he had vanished into thin air! There was absolutely nowhere that he could have secreted himself. The men searched high and low and with great care but they found no trace of him. Completely baffled, they knew they hadn't been seeing things. To this day, this mysterious appearance and disappearance has never been explained.

Govan Depot used to have the reputation of being haunted by a ghostly figure which seemed to like to climb into the driving cabs of the Subway cars. Obviously a stranger in such a place had to be investigated, but, try as they might, the night workers could never actually catch him at it because, just like the previous gentleman with the raincoat and flat cap, he simply evaporated. However, when his pursuers entered the driver's cab where he had been spotted, they always found it empty and much, much colder than its surroundings. Icily and unnaturally so.

Other unexplained phenomena on the Glasgow Subway include mysterious noises like the repeated sound of a hammer hitting a rail between St Enoch and Bridge Street stations when maintenance work was being done at night. Also there used to be what are described as singing noises, for all the world like a female choir, heard by night-time cleaners working in the tunnels between Kelvinbridge and Hillhead stations where the line is quite deep underground.

Pinwherry

Pinwherry is a wayside station on the long secondary main line from Girvan to Stranraer. The line was built by the Girvan & Portpatrick Railway and opened in 1870. It met the Portpatrick & Wigtownshire joint line from Dumfries at Challoch Junction and had running powers over its line through Stranraer to Portpatrick.

Shields Road Station at platform level. This is an ill-frequented station on the 'Clockwork Orange', Glasgow's subway system.

A story, amusing rather than paranormal, is told about Pinwherry. One night an exceptionally heavy southbound freight train was scheduled from Girvan to Stranraer. The only locomotive available was a small and under-powered one. It was obvious that it could not tackle the 1 in 54 gradient of Glendoune Bank with the whole train so a decision was taken to divide the train and take half as far as Pinmore. The locomotive would then return to Girvan and hook up with the second half of the train, bring it to Pinmore where the two halves could be united and taken over the easier gradients on to Stranraer. The first section was worked through to Pinmore and the loco-motive detached as planned. However, before the brakes on the wagons could be pinned down, they began to move down the incline they had just come up, gathering speed as they went. Luckily there were no other trains expected as these wagons almost joyfully rushed down through Pinwherry. The sta-tion there was in a dip after which the line climbed towards Girvan. This gradient slowed them down and they eventually halted for a second before gravity took over and back they hurtled through Pinwherry once more. They continued to roll to and fro at least six times, slowly losing momentum before coming to a rest close to Pinwherry Station. A permanent way inspector was lodging for the night in the stationmaster's house and at breakfast next morning he was rather grumpy. He had hardly had a wink all night, he said,

Pinwherry; the scene of a restless night for the inspector staying in the station house.

because trains were hurtling through the station every few minutes. Never, he stated, in over twenty years service on the railways, had he ever known such a busy country station. It's just as well he didn't look out of the window or he may well have seen a ghost train with wagons but no locomotive rushing past.

The line from Girvan to Stranraer is still operational. At Pinmore, incidentally, the ghost of a woman who threw herself under a train has been seen from time to time.

The Tay Bridge

The River Tay has its source in a corrie on the slopes of Ben Lui in the Grampians, and it flows 110 miles to pass Dundee and enter the sea. Dundee had become a major industrial centre by the nineteenth century, but it was finding the Firth of Tay a formidable natural barrier to the development of its industries, the famous 'three J's' – jute, jam and journalism. Until the 1860s the received wisdom was that the Firth was so wide that there was no possibility of a bridge being built across it in the vicinity of Dundee.

That there was a need for a bridge across the Tay cannot be denied. To journey the mere forty-six miles from Edinburgh involved the traveller having a strong stomach, a stoical lack of imagination and plenty of time; well over three hours or more when there were any of the frequent storms on the Forth and the Tay. From Edinburgh Waverley the train trundled the short distance to

Granton where the passengers boarded a ferry and lurched dyspeptically across the Forth to Burntisland. There a train waited to take them to Newport on the south side of the Tay where the woebegone travellers embarked on a second ferry and crossed the Firth to Broughty Ferry from where yet a third train waited to take them the short distance to Dundee.

The prize for the railway company that built a bridge across the Tay would be a rich one and the benefits for Dundonians would be enormous. A bridge would need to be two miles long, and no bridge on this scale had ever been built. It would be an object of enormous pride for the citizens of Dundee, giving the city the direct route to the south that it desperately needed and thereby putting the city firmly on the national map. The North British Railway Co. decided to grasp the nettle and they engaged Thomas Bouch, an experienced builder of railway structures, as its engineer. Work started on 22 July 1871. To ensure sufficient headroom for shipping on the Tay, the rails would pass through the most elevated central part of the bridge in what became known as the 'High Girders'. On the rest of the bridge the rails would run along the top of box girders.

As the bridge began to take shape, distinguished visitors came to gaze at this new wonder of the world. These included the old King of Brazil who got so carried away that he argued for a similar but somewhat longer bridge to be built across the mouth of the Amazon! Prince Leopold of Prussia was another royal, but the most popular celebrity seems to have been General Ulysses Simpson Grant, eighteenth President of the USA and a hero of the Union Army. His nickname was 'Old Glory', and the crowds gave him a marvellous reception, but despite his swashbuckling reputation it soon became obvious that whenever he was asked a question it was always his wife who answered it. The only time he managed to forestall her was when he was canvassed for his opinion of the bridge. 'It's a very long bridge,' he said. This rather dull statement accorded with the generally accepted view that Grant was the strong and silent sort, but it still elicited a cheer from the crowd if only because it was the first time any of them had actually heard the general speak.

The first train to cross this prodigious bridge was a 'directors' special' which did so on 26 September 1877. The bridge still had to undergo examination by an inspecting officer from the Royal Engineers on behalf of the Board of Trade before it could be passed as fit to carry fare-paying passengers. The inspector was the very model of a modern major-general by the name of Charles Scrope Hutchinson. He was a meticulous and incorruptible man who spent three days examining the bridge minutely, walking it from end to end, travelling over it on a special train, poking about under it in a boat and even surveying it from a distance with a telescope and finally a theodolite. He passed the bridge as fit for public use with the proviso of a speed limit of 25mph. He added what in retrospect was an ominous rider to his report. These were his words: 'I should wish, if possible, to have an opportunity of observing the effects of a high wind when a train of carriages is running over the bridge.'

This caveat not withstanding, Dundee was en fête. Bouch was the hero of the day, fit to stand in the pantheon of British heroes alongside the likes of Drake, the Duke of Marlborough and Nelson. Bathing in this popular adulation, Bouch was already engaged in preliminary work for a bridge across the Firth of Forth to replace the Granton to Burntisland ferry. The Queen visited Dundee, took a trip across the bridge and knighted Bouch. On that day the city's schoolchildren were given a day off, and the dear little weans were soon sinking their fangs into 'Tay Bridge Rock', each and every one of them having been presented with this sticky sweetmeat as a memento of the occasion. As sweetmeats they were greatly appreciated. As souvenirs, they were a complete failure.

It was soon obvious that not all was well with the bridge. Trains were crossing it at speeds considerably in excess of the prescribed 25mph, maintenance men were noticing a disconcerting number of bolts and rivets which had worked loose, and they also talked about the excessive vibration which occurred when trains passed over the bridge, especially if they were going too fast.

On Sunday 28 December 1879 an appalling storm was causing structural damage in Dundee and whipping the waters of the Tay into waves that hit the piers of the bridge with sufficient force to produce spray and spindrift that the wind flung over the trains far above. It was truly a terrifying tempest. The awesome power of the wind brought people out to gaze at the churned-up waters of the Tay, and all averred they had never seen a storm like it. The bridge was still a major talking-point with Dundonians and inevitably people watched with fascination as the last trains of the day made their way across. Sparks and flashes were to be seen as the trains moved through the 'High Girders'. Perhaps they were red-hot coals from the locomotives' fireboxes. It became evident later that the cause of at least some of them was the friction created on the wheel flanges and on the rails when the trains were hit by especially powerful gusts as they were passing through the 'High Girders'.

The very last train of the day was the 5.20 p.m. from Burntisland, and several people were watching its progress across the bridge when there was a sudden flurry of flashes just as the moon emerged and suffused the firth in silvery light. To their horror, the watchers saw that there was a breach in the High Girders. The bridge was down!

The train had been hit by an extra-strong gust of wind, perhaps as much as 110mph, when it was within the girders, a section of which was dislodged, whereupon it fell into the icy waters below. All the seventy-five passengers thought to be on board drowned and the bodies of twenty-nine of them were never recovered. The train stayed remarkably intact, having been protected from damage by the ironwork of the girders themselves.

The locomotive was a 4-4-0, North British No.224, and she was so little damaged by her submarine adventure that she was recovered, repaired and returned to traffic. However, she never ventured across the Tay Bridge after it was rebuilt. The North British Co. thought it sensible to roster No.224 for duties elsewhere. Besides, it was quite possible that superstitious footplatemen would refuse to work it over the bridge as it was thought of as a 'jinxed' locomotive, although only in that particular location. Its exploits earned it the nickname 'The Diver'.

Ever since that fateful night at the end of 1879, people on the anniversary claim to have seen a ghostly steam train crossing the bridge from the Fife

The Tay Bridge shortly after it opened. The 'High Girders' which collapsed, carrying the train with them, can be seen.

The 'High Girders' have gone!

A view of the missing section of Tay Bridge.

SIR THOMAS BOUCH
CIVIL ENGINEER
BORN 25 FEB. 1822
DIED 30 OCT. 1880

Sir Thomas Bouch bore the brunt of the criticism for the collapse of the Tay Bridge. Revisionist historians think he was made a scapegoat. This is his memorial in Dean Cemetery, Edinburgh.

end and suddenly disappearing from sight with sparks and flashes galore. This kind of supernatural experience is often referred to as a re-enactment haunting and is not uncommon where events involving extreme emotions have taken place. A dispassionate view would be that such a thing was simply impossible. However, there has been a constant procession of people who have come forward claiming to have seen this spectral train on the night in question.

More static ghosts are some of the piers of Bouch's ill-fated bridge, many of which can still be seen from the Fife or southern shore protruding from the river and alongside the replacement bridge.

The Waverley Route

Without a doubt one of Britain's most fabled main lines was the Waverley Route, so-called because the line passed near Abbotsford, the home of the once very popular novelist, Sir Walter Scott. His prolific output of loosely historical novels had started with *Waverley*, published in 1814. It would not be unfair to say that this line has generated an interest out of all proportion to its former importance as a part of the country's railway network. Perhaps its fascination is wrapped up with the nature of the terrain it traversed. Once it was beyond the outer environs of Edinburgh, the route passed through largely empty and remote countryside and through hills whose gradients provided a stern test for the mettle of locomotives and footplatemen. With good reason the local drivers and firemen called it 'The Long Line'.

Also, this was once the territory of the Border Reivers. These were the people who, 400 years ago and less, gave the world a preview of organised gangsterism as they roamed the bleak countryside feuding, raiding, extorting and engaging in family vendettas and almost always doing so with complete immunity from authority. Something of the emotionally charged atmosphere their activities created still clings to the windswept fells and dales of this beautiful but harsh countryside. A few miles from the line and not far from the present Hawick to Newcastleton road stands Hermitage Castle. Is there any equally desolate spot in Britain containing such a sinister-looking building? Hermitage was associated with Lord Soulis, a fiend in human form capable of every form of atrocity and wickedness. His activities were recalled in verse, a fragment of which gives a flavour:

The axe he bears, it hacks and tears,
'Tis form'd of an earth-fast flint;
No armour of knight, tho' ever so wight,
Can bear its deadly dint.

No danger he fears, for a charmed sword he wears,
Of adderstone the hilt:

No Tynedale knight had ever such might,
But his heart-blood was spilt.

The origins of the line date back to 1845 when the North British Railway Co. obtained powers to build a line from Edinburgh to Hawick, and this opened in 1849. The hills through which the line passed supported vast numbers of sheep. The pure water which tumbled off the fells was excellent for processing the raw wool which was then worked up in towns like Galashiels and Hawick into high-quality material generically known as 'tweed'. The North British saw good business in supporting the expansion of the woollen industry in this area not least by being able to bring in cheap coal from the Lothian coalfield to power the mill furnaces.

By the time the line had reached Hawick, that town was no longer the ultimate goal. The North British now had Carlisle in its sights. There was an awful lot of barren moorland in the forty-three miles from Hawick to Carlisle, with heavy engineering works and little possibility of much intermediate originating traffic. The border city was only reached in 1862 and the southern end was a financial liability, built like a main line but only earning frugal branch line revenue until 1876.

In that year the English-based Midland Railway reached Carlisle with its own independent line from Settle and Leeds. There was little love lost between the North British and Midland railway companies serving Carlisle on the one hand and the Caledonian and London & North Western companies on the other. The former companies now had between them a through route from Edinburgh to London (St Pancras) via Leeds. The Midland had an arrangement with the Glasgow & South Western Railway Co. whereby traffic from Glasgow via Kilmarnock and Dumfries could also be channelled via the Settle and Carlisle line to Leeds, the East Midlands and London. This meant that the Waverley route now became part of a trunk Anglo-Scottish facility, and so it assumed a new identity as an important main line.

The dramatic countryside through which the Waverley route passes has for long attracted railway photographers. Early in the 1950s one such photographer decided to spend a day in the vicinity of Shankend. This had a minor and ill-frequented station just south of Hawick, and at one time a fine mansion had stood on the hillside overlooking the line. By this time it had been abandoned and was a derelict and forbidding hulk surrounded by policies which had become wild and overgrown. Wherever you were in the Shankend area, somehow it was impossible to ignore the presence of this brooding relic.

The photographer was an old hand, well-used to carting his equipment across fields and through thickets in his search for the best lineside locations, but Shankend was new to him. This time it wasn't impenetrable brambles or fast-flowing streams that put him off but a horribly threatening sense of an unseen malignant presence. So real was the apprehension that he felt, even on this sunny summer's day, that he decided to leave without having taken even a single picture. He could not help thinking that if the place was so threatening on a day like that, it could only be a thousand times more so on a grey and gloomy November afternoon. What would it be like in the witching hours?

Later he talked to fellow railway photographers and those who had been to the Shankend area all agreed that there was indeed something horrible about the atmosphere there. Two of them said that they would never return. Enquiries established that the big house had been requisitioned for use as a prisoner-of-war camp during the First World War. The inmates suffered an appalling visitation of typhoid, sometimes called 'gaol fever', and the victims had been buried in graves scattered around the policies close to the house. When the war was over the house was put out to rent, but those who moved in quickly moved out. The place got a bad name, became hard to let and eventually was left vacant and fell into disrepair. Was it the ghosts of the POWs that exuded the air of menace around Shankend?

It may well have been the presence of the same former prisoner-of-war camp that spoiled the efforts of a well-known recorder of railway sounds. Trains worked hard up the gradient near Shankend and made an ideal subject for sound recording. The recorder stood close to the lineside, having found what he thought was the ideal spot. His hobby required patience and fortitude but as he waited in the dark he knew it was wise not to allow his imagination too full a rein in a spot as bleak and remote as this. At last he heard a distant lonesome whistle and the sound of a labouring locomotive which heralded the approach of a suitable subject for a recording. He got his equipment ready when he became aware of strange, rather eerie noises coming from a nearby copse. A trifle put out but not daunted by this unwelcome sound, he tried to switch the recorder on but one of the tapes jammed just at the critical moment. The train heaved itself up the hill, approaching and then passing with a crescendo of just the kind of sounds he wanted to record for posterity. He fiddled impotently with his recorder but it was no good. That was one train that got away. Somewhat mortified, he decided to call it a day. As the sound of the hard-working engine reverberated from the surrounding hills and gradually faded away, he became aware that it was as black as Newgate Knocker, that he was very much alone and there had been those strange sounds coming from somewhere close by. Fortunately they had stopped, but it had suddenly become colder.

He was clearly a man of resource, however, because early next morning he returned to the same location, not to do any recording but to investigate the little wood from which the unnerving sounds had come. Under the trees were small iron markers recording the burial places of Germans who had died in the typhoid outbreak at the nearby prison camp.

One of the most extraordinary places on the Waverley Route was Riccarton Junction, not very far south of Shankend, where the route met a line known as the Border Counties Railway, which had opened at the same time. This railway backwater meandered southwards through hopelessly empty country with few settlements of any size until it reached the valley of the North Tyne. At Hexham it joined up with the North Eastern Railway's Newcastle–Carlisle line.

Riccarton Junction was an exceptionally desolate and isolated spot on an exposed hillside about fifteen miles south of Hawick and a considerable distance from any road. For that reason Riccarton Junction was totally dependent on the railway for its communications with the outside world. The community there had been created by the North British Railway as a depot for the small locomotives that spent their lives 'banking'. This involved the locomotives attaching themselves to the rear of trains and shoving them by brute force up to and over Whitrope Summit. There was also a depot where the various engineering materials and tools were kept to maintain the track and other equipment in the area. The company built thirty cottages to house the railway workers and their families. There was a co-op shop, a sub post office, a refreshment room, a one-teacher infant and junior school and a social club in the station yard. On alternate Sundays, a couple of local trains stopped to pick up any of the residents who wanted to worship in either Hawick or Newcastleton, but there were never many takers.

To be honest few of the North British's employees volunteered for duties at Riccarton Junction. The truth was that many of the workers there had been sent, often for disciplinary reasons, to a place regarded as a punishment, a kind of 'sin bin' where they could perhaps do the least damage. Given its isolation, this meant that the settlement resembled nothing so much as a lawless frontier town in the Wild West. Rumours circulated about an outbreak of incest at Riccarton Junction and of riotous communal orgies, and a company official was despatched to investigate. Perhaps to his disappointment he found no particular evidence of sexual irregularities but reported that the village was effectively being run by a gang of four women who made life an absolute hell for anyone to whom they took a dislike. It was serious enough that the procurator-fiscal and the police became involved, but although they sent the formidable viragos concerned on their way, Riccarton Junction continued to have a reputation for lawlessness.

In such a necessarily self-contained community it was of course inevitable that from time to time the residents would get on each others' nerves, but some relief was offered on a Saturday when a late afternoon train called which some of them used to travel southwards to Newcastleton. The goal was the *Grapes Inn*. There was no return train and so the sozzled revellers had little option but to walk the eight or more miles in the cess alongside the railway track. It was only to be expected that there were several near-misses over the years, and the company officially frowned on the practice.

The line witnessed an extremely unpleasant outbreak of racial violence among the railway labourers employed in construction work in the Gorebridge area south of Dalkeith. The Irish workers on the site had a grievance about their pay and they retired in high dudgeon to a local pub to drown their sorrows. An itinerant peddler was trying to sell watches and handed two round for prospective buyers to look at. They were seized by the navvies who refused to hand them back, and then things turned nasty. Two Irishmen were arrested only for a large number of others to force the police to give them up. The navvies were triumphant but still angry when they came across a couple more police officers on their way to the scene. A fight broke out during which one of the officers received fatal injuries.

This incident incensed the Scottish and English navvies working locally and a large force forced the Irish to retreat and then ransacked and destroyed their encampment, this being done, so it was alleged, while the police looked the other way. The word got around, the Irish calling up reinforcements, and an uneasy peace was only restored after troops were called out. The unfortunate police officer was buried in Borthwick Kirkyard, but it appears that his spirit refused to take things lying down and that he was frequently seen, in the form of a police officer wearing an early style of uniform, wandering restlessly in the vicinity of these tragic events. He has not been seen since the line closed.

The proposal to close the line was one of the most controversial in Dr Beeching's package of changes with which he hoped would make the railways pay their way. The line closed on the first weekend of January 1969

Fine Art Deco relief sculpture decorating the LMSR side of Leeds City Station.

amid warnings that lineside bombs were due to be detonated as the last train went past. At Hawick a party dressed as undertakers boarded the train carrying a coffin inscribed: 'Waverley Line, born 1849, killed 1969. Aged 120 years.' At Newcastleton the locals, led by the vicar, staged a sit-down strike which further delayed the already very late last train.

With a detailed map, a compass, stout walking boots and the right clothes, parts of the line can still be followed today by those with a rugged constitution and determined disposition. Some of the splendid viaducts and earthworks can be viewed from the windows of their cars by those who prefer their creature comforts. The only trains that pass now are, of course, ghost trains.

GHOSTS OF THE LONDON UNDERGROUND

The Metropolitan Railway opened for business on 10 January 1863 with 30,000 passengers on the first day, and was viewed as an engineering marvel at the time. It was the first underground railway in the world and it ran from Bishop's Road at Paddington to Farringdon. With over 270 stations and 253 miles of track carrying millions of people every year, the London Underground system is predictably crowded, claustrophobic and at times uncomfortable. However, it is also a defining part of London's identity, recognisable by its distinctive logo, map and architecture, and it has served the transport needs of the capital for nearly 150 years.

Not surprisingly it has inspired many stories, and anyone who has stood on a platform on an Underground station late at night will appreciate what an eerie place it can be with its labyrinth of subterranean tunnels and passages and just a hint that unseen entities may be lurking down there. As with the main line railway system, the Underground has experienced various closures and has its share of abandoned stations. As a train speeds along, passengers may catch a glimpse of one of the fabled 'ghost stations', the train's bright lights reflecting off begrimed tiling on the platform. The building of and exten-sion to parts of the system have entailed encroaching on old burial grounds and plague pits, and again ghost stories have arisen in connection with these. Ghosts do not take kindly to being disturbed.

Over the years, staff who work on the Underground at night have often reported strange incidents such as unexplained noises and sightings, sudden and sharp drops in temperature, creepy feelings of unease and even sightings of people who had died years earlier, sometimes in accidents on the line. Both staff and passengers have reported phenomena which include a faceless woman, a 7ft human figure, the ghosts of actors, a woman in black, the dreadful screams of a thirteen-year-old girl who was murdered in the eighteenth century, reflections in carriage windows of someone not corporeally there, screams of women and children who were crushed to death in a disaster during the Second World War, semi-transparent apparitions, tales of troglodytes and even a screaming Egyptian mummy.

THE DEVELOPMENT OF THE LONDON UNDERGROUND

The 'Underground' is actually something of a misnomer because only about 42 per cent of the system actually runs below the surface. The network grew up, at least until the early 1930s, in a largely piecemeal fashion, but it has evolved to become an essential part of the capital's infrastructure. The need for the system originated with the chronic road traffic gridlock which had developed on the surface by the middle of the nineteenth century.

The line that ran the four miles from Paddington to Farringdon, going on to form the nucleus of the Metropolitan Railway, was built just below street level using what became known as the 'cut-and-cover' method. This method may have caused temporary chaos for traffic but it reduced the potential costs involved in the compulsory purchase of many of the buildings that lay on or around the path of the projected route. Steam locomotives hauled the early trains and, because the line was in a relatively shallow trench open to the air for much of the route, some of the smoke and steam dissipated. However, the poisonous and almost impenetrable fug in stations such as Baker Street, which were entirely subterranean, caused travellers to cough, splutter and complain, and for this reason early underground train travel was certainly not for the faint-hearted. The smoky atmosphere of the stations and the dimly-lit trains provided a fruitful field of operation for the light-fingered criminal fraternity.

In spite of apocalyptic predictions that the building of underground railways would disturb the Devil who would then wreak his revenge on those foolish enough to travel on subterranean lines, the route from Paddington to Farringdon was an almost total success. This stimulated further development and other lines followed. The building of these lines prompted urban development and a complex network of lines was created linking suburban and rural areas to the city and to Central London. There was no sense of the

This statue of Sir John Betjeman at St Pancras depicts the poet with his trademark shopping bag gazing up in awe at the station's magnificent cast-iron roof, the widest in Britain.

need to create a co-ordinated system between the companies that developed the early lines and so some parts of Greater London, particularly south of the Thames, have always been distant from the Tube although they usually came to be served adequately by the impressive network of surface electrified lines which we tend to associate with the Southern Railway Co. In 1933 control of a unified underground system passed into the hands of the London Passenger Transport Board which set about a programme of extensions to the tube system and modernisation of rolling stock, stations and other facilities. Developments since the war have been few and slow in coming, but the Victoria Line, opened throughout in 1972, and the Jubilee Line Extension in 1999 have set new standards for automation and efficient operation.

Without question the London Underground has had an enormous social, economic and cultural impact on the metropolis. It has provided a ready means for people to get around quickly and easily, it has connected the disparate collection of 'villages' which constitutes London and stimulated the growth of vast tracts of London's inner and more distant suburbia including, of course, the 'Metroland' affectionately mocked by Sir John Betjeman (1906–84). In addition, the Underground has assisted the regeneration of areas of inner-city decay such as the Bermondsey district of south-east London with, in this case, the building of the Jubilee Line. The Underground has given the world the immortal diagrammatic map of the system, originated by Harry Beck in 1932. It has expressed itself in stations of the highest architectural merit such as Park Royal and East Finchley and the monumental headquarters block of 55 Broadway Street with its sculptures by Henry Moore and Jacob Epstein. It has also given us the distinctive glazed terracotta station fronts which are the colour of oxblood and the Art and Crafts faience work of the architect Leslie W. Green. The deep-level tubes played a heroic role sheltering Londoners during the Blitz. Elsewhere some stations and unopened tube tunnels were used as subterranean factories producing such things as aircraft parts. Others became control centres for the war effort. The Underground is absolutely a part of London's fabric. Life would be very different without it, and much worse.

There has of course also been a debit side. The building of the sub-surface lines was extraordinarily disruptive and often meant that people lost their homes, most frequently those who could not afford expensive legal counsel to contest compulsory purchase orders. Many burial sites had to be disturbed and human remains laid to rest elsewhere, something about which many people were uneasy. The Underground has had its share of drama including murders, suicides, tragic accidents and, more recently, terrorist bomb attacks.

London's many disused underground stations generate growing interest. These 'ghost stations' with their long-abandoned platforms, cold, darkened tunnels and the nagging suggestion that something horrible might be lurking down there provide ideal settings for reports of hauntings and paranormal phenomena. Even many of the stations still in regular use are spooky first thing in the morning and last thing at night when few passengers are about and trains less frequent. What happens on the platforms and in the passages when no living entities are there? The deep-level tube stations in particular contain doors sealed off to access by the general public. What secrets do those doors conceal?

HAUNTED UNDERGROUND STATIONS

There are many reputedly haunted Underground stations and lines. For example, in the 1960s and '70s many motormen dreaded being held up by signals on the section between Holborn and Chancery Lane. Workers reported that when their trains drew to a halt at adverse signals they would suddenly become aware that in the partial light shed by the carriage lights behind them they were sharing the driving cab with an uninvited guest. This indistinct figure was apparently staring fixedly ahead through the cab front windows and standing just a foot or two away from them. As soon as the train moved off when the signals changed, the figure vanished.

Other haunted stations include Becontree where, in 1992, the ghost of a faceless woman with blonde hair was seen standing on the platform. Commuters and staff at the Elephant & Castle Underground Station have seen a young lone female late at night entering the carriage of a tube train and then inexplicably vanishing. At Hyde Park Corner in the early 1970s two maintenance workers on the night shift were amazed to hear the sound of the escalator in motion, given that they had just switched the power off. There was no living being there to turn the power back on. In 1951 an electrician was engaged in maintenance work on the platform at Ickenham Station when he saw the ghost of a middle-aged woman dressed in old-fashioned clothing. The woman, who gestured for him to follow her, was believed to have fallen from the platform and been electrocuted many years earlier. Several witnesses have talked about feeling the presence of invisible hands at Maida Vale Station as they were coming up the escalators from platform to street level. In the 1980s at Queensbury the figure of Sir Winston Churchill was allegedly seen on the platform, apparently waiting for a train.

Elephant & Castle Station. Although these underground passages are well-lit, they can be eerie and menacing early in the morning or last thing at night when few people are about.

Train crews on trains have seen an indistinct figure on the line from Baker Street as it approaches Rickmansworth. In 1928 a passenger alighting from the last train at South Kensington found himself alone on the platform whereupon he reported having seen a spectral steam locomotive on the track with the figure of a man standing next to it. An old-fashioned-looking workman reputedly haunts the tunnels around Stockwell. It is believed he was a track worker who was killed by a train on this stretch of line sometime in the 1950s. In the 1990s there were a number of sightings of what was described as a 'semi-transparent' apparition walking by the side of the four-track section of line close to Turnham Green Station. At West Brompton Underground Station the ghost of a late Victorian or Edwardian workman strides out purposefully before vanishing.

What follows is a selection of London Underground stations where experiences of supernatural activity have been reported. Some of these cases are reasonably well known, others less so (readers may wish to look at a more detailed account by the authors in *The Haunted London Underground* published in 2008 by The History Press).

ALDGATE

Aldgate Station dates from 1876 and is on the Circle Line between Tower Hill and Liverpool Street as well as being the eastern terminus of the Metropolitan Line. It famously features in one of the Sherlock Holmes stories, *The Bruce-Partington Plans*, and in September 1888 the Jack the Ripper victim Catherine Eddowes was murdered nearby in Mitre Square. The station was badly damaged by German bombs during the Second World War, and in July 2005 one of the four of the London suicide bombings exploded on a Circle Line train as it left Liverpool Street and was approaching Aldgate Station, killing seven innocent people and inflicting awful injuries on others.

Aldgate Station was built immediately next door to St Botolph's Church which contains the site of one of the biggest plague pits in London, where over 1,000 plague victims were buried in the graveyard in the space of just two weeks in September 1665. Altogether over 4,000 bodies were buried at Aldgate. Daniel Defoe, in his *A Journal of the Plague Year*, described the gruesome horrors at Aldgate:

> ... they dug the great pit in the churchyard of our parish of Aldgate. A terrible pit it was, and I could not resist my curiosity to go and see it. As near as I may judge, it was about forty feet in length, and about fifteen or sixteen feet broad, and at the time I first looked at it, about nine feet deep; but it was said they dug it near twenty feet deep afterwards in one part of it... Into these pits they had put perhaps fifty or sixty bodies each; then they made larger holes wherein they buried all that the cart brought in a week... At the beginning of September, the plague raging in a dreadful manner, and the number of burials in our parish increasing to more than was ever buried in any parish about London... they ordered this dreadful gulf to be dug – for such it was, rather than a pit...the pit being finished the 4th of September, I think, they began to bury in it the 6th, and by the 20th, which was just two weeks, they had thrown into it 1,114 bodies when they were obliged to fill it up.

A well-known story relating to the station concerns a track worker who was working a late shift at the station a few years ago. The man suddenly slipped as he bent over the rails and came into contact with the 20,000-volt conductor rail, which caused a massive surge of electricity to pass through his body. The shock knocked him unconscious and he was fortunate not to be killed. One of his co-workers nearby saw the incident but also witnessed a most eerie sight. Just seconds before the man touched the live rail his colleague saw the figure of a half-transparent old woman gently stroking the man's hair. The old woman was believed to have been killed during the Second World War by falling onto a similar rail.

Passengers have reported other unexplained occurrences such as the sound of footsteps in the early hours of the morning although there has been no

Aldgate Station opened in 1876 on the Metropolitan Line and was extensively rebuilt at street level in the mid-1920s.

visible sign of anyone, and also strange and mournful whistling. The latter appears to be a common occurrence on the Underground and one explanation suggests this is due to the presence of infrasound – sound with a frequency too low to be heard by human ear.

Two psychologists at Coventry University, Vic Tandy and Tony Lawrence, wrote a paper called 'Ghosts in the Machine' for the journal of the Society for Psychical Research. Tandy appeared on a Channel 5 programme, *Ghosts on the Underground* (2006), in order to examine phenomena at London Underground stations where high levels of supernatural activity had been recorded. One of their conclusions was that escalator motors, moving trains or wind from the tunnels can produce distorted sounds, particularly on deep-level tube stations, which may give rise to some of the stories about spooky phenomena.

ALDWYCH

Aldwych is a disused station and therefore could also justifiably be described as a ghost station. The station has been used as the location for TV and film productions such as *Death Line* (1972); *V for Vendetta* (2006); *Atonement* (2007);

and the horror film *Creep* (2004). The TV programme *Most Haunted* devoted a whole programme to Aldwych in 2002.

Aldwych was formerly on the Piccadilly Line and was the terminus of a short branch from Holborn until it was closed in September 1994. It is located on the Strand and was opened as the Strand Station (it changed its name to Aldwych in 1917) in November 1907, running a shuttle service for city workers and for theatre-goers. During the Second World War the branch was closed with the operational platform being used as a public air-raid shelter, and the disused platform and running tunnel were commandeered to house some of the valuable artifacts from the British Museum, including the Elgin Marbles. The station has two entrances – one on the Strand and another around the corner on Surrey Street. Both are instantly recognisable for what they are or were.

Aldwych Station was built on the site of the Royal Strand Theatre, which was demolished to make way for it. One of the ghosts is associated with the theatre and has been seen lurking around the station platform. The Royal Strand Theatre went through various changes of name and renovations during its history, but it finally closed on 13 May 1905. The female ghost that haunts the station is rumoured to be that of an actress who did not enjoy her last curtain call. 'Fluffers', the workers who used to clean the accumulation of dust from the tunnels, particularly the human hair and skin cells, reported being scared by a figure, possibly female, who appeared on the tracks at night in the vicinity of Aldwych tube. Who is the ghostly actress? There are a number of contenders. Some say it may be one of the female cast involved in the last show staged at the theatre, *Miss Wingrove*. It was not a success and closed down abruptly after only a week. Equally, it could have been any one of the many actresses who appeared in the seventy years of the theatre's history.

The TV series *Most Haunted* failed to cast any further light on the mystery although they acknowledged that Aldwych did seem to have a particularly high level of paranormal activity. The team suggested that there were two female and one male ghost. The name Margaret was mentioned with a possible middle name or other name of Estelle and a surname sounding like Bryce or Bright.

We can only speculate at the identity of the actress. Frances 'Fanny' Kelly (1790–1882) opened at the Strand in February 1833 in which she was advertised as playing twenty different characters. Frances makes for a likely candidate especially because some descriptions of the Aldwych ghost said she appeared in many guises! Although Fanny Kelly was successful elsewhere, she failed at the Strand. She was the first to devise and perform a one-woman show, and when she retired from the stage in the 1830s she founded a drama school for women in Dean Street, Soho. Her popularity on stage brought her many admirers. On two occasions, in London and Dublin, two different men tried to shoot her whilst she was on stage! Sadly she lived out her later years in relative poverty and died just before receiving a monetary prize associated with the Literary

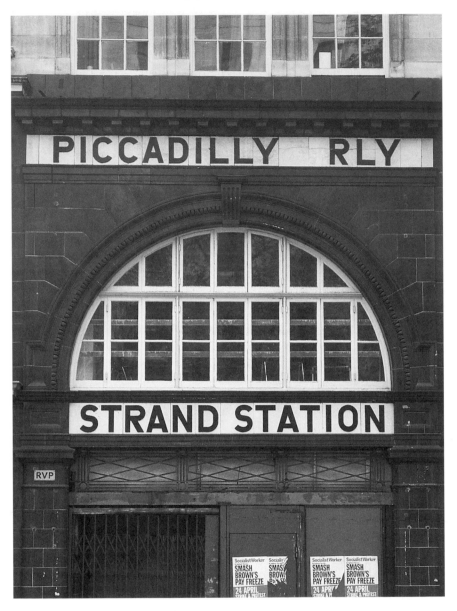

The Strand Entrance to the closed Aldwych Tube Station. No, you're not seeing things! The station was opened in 1907 as 'Strand', and was renamed 'Aldwych' in 1915. For much of the Second World War Aldwych was used by Westminster City Council as a public air-raid shelter.

The Surrey Street entrance to the former Aldwych Tube Station.

Fund award conferred on her by Queen Victoria. Did she ever get over her failure at the Royal Strand Theatre?

It might well be that the ghost was a lesser-known figure who never quite made a career on stage but who looks desperately for applause or that elusive last curtain call.

BAKERLOO LINE

In the area of Elephant & Castle and various other Bakerloo Line stations, especially Baker Street, there have been many reports from passengers who were sitting and gazing into space only to look up and catch a glimpse of the reflection of another passenger sitting next to them. This would be all well and good except that the passengers making these reports were sitting at the time with unoccupied seats on either side of them! The vast majority of such reports concern trains going northwards. The Bakerloo is not unique in producing this strange phenomenon, but none of the other lines can compete with it for the number of occasions on which travellers claim to have had this rather disconcerting experience. The nearest rival seems to be the Piccadilly Line, near Earl's Court.

A variation on this theme is for the reflection to be that of a figure dressed in the clothes of a bygone era.

BANK

Bank Monument is one of the largest and most complex subterranean railway stations in the world. The station, which is named after the nearby Bank of England on Threadneedle Street, was opened in 1900 for the Central London Railway whilst Monument Station had been completed for the (Inner) Circle Line about 100 yards away in 1884. The City and South London Railway (later part of the Northern Line) tried to save on costs by excavating beneath St Mary Woolnoth Church to build the lift-shafts and station. After much objection the railway company bought the crypt for what is now the Northern Line booking hall, so the entrance that once led to the crypt now leads into Bank Underground Station. The bones of the dead were moved for reburial at the City of London Cemetery at Ilford in 1900.

Bank Station received a direct hit by a bomb in January 1941. It penetrated the road surface and exploded in an escalator machinery room killing fifty-six people and injuring sixty-nine. In 1982, as the station was closing, a worker who was walking across the ticket hall heard a banging coming from inside the lift despite the fact that he just checked it and knew that there was no one else around.

The most famous ghost associated with the station as well as the nearby Bank of England is reputedly that of Sarah Whitehead who has gained the nickname of the 'Bank Nun' (or in some cases the 'Black Nun'). Construction workers building that part of the Underground first saw her in the late nineteenth century. Some years later a member of staff chased what he thought was an old lady locked in the station during the early hours of the morning. Just as he thought he had caught her up she disappeared down a corridor with no possible exit. Some years later an employee reported seeing a female figure which suddenly vanished. There have been further sightings up to recent times of the ghost of Sarah desperately searching for something or somebody.

The story of Sarah goes back to 1811 when her brother was charged with forgery and brought before the Old Bailey to stand trial. Her brother, Philip Whitehead, who is referred to as 'Paul' at the trial on 30 October 1811, was a former employee at the Bank of England. Whitehead had worked as a clerk in the cashier's office at the bank but had resigned from his job on 2 August 1810. The crimes with which he was charged were against a number of businessmen and not the bank itself. The law took a very grave view of forgery and it was an offence for which the penalty was mandatory – judicial hanging.

And so it was with Paul. At the age of thirty-six he was sentenced to death and subsequently executed.

His devoted sister Sarah had been taken to a house in Fleet Street and protected from all news of her brother. Anxious to find out about his whereabouts she set off to the Bank of England where a clerk who, presumably not knowing who she was, blurted out that her brother had received the death sentence. Stunned and shocked by this news, Sarah could not come to terms with what she had been told and it clearly affected her mind. Shortly after she took to visiting the bank on a regular basis dressed in black crêpe, veil and long dress, still asking for her brother. The staff nicknamed her the 'Bank Nun', but her visits were a source of pity as well as a nuisance to the bank. Staff and customers were made uneasy by her brooding presence.

Despite the bank trying to come to a financial arrangement whereby she would agree to stop hanging around the building, Sarah continued with her visits and loitered near the entrance consistently over the period between 1812 and 1837, attired in a heavy mourning dress which contrasted strangely with her painted cheeks. Her ghost, also dressed in black, was heard to be asking 'has anyone seen my brother?' Sarah was reputedly buried in the old churchyard of St Christopher-le-Stocks, which afterwards became part of the bank's gardens.

Bank of England. The 'Old Lady of Threadneedle Street' is a refashioning of a Palladian building originally erected in 1734.

This is only one of several entrances to Bank Station, but it gives little idea of the extensive and confusing complex of passages below.

BETHNAL GREEN

Bethnal Green Station, which is on the Central Line between Liverpool Street and Mile End stations, was the scene of the worst civilian disaster of the Second World War. The East End of London had experienced heavy bombing raids during the war, but on 3 March 1943, 173 people (twenty-seven men, eighty-four women and sixty-two children) were killed and ninety-two injured in a crush whilst attempting to enter the station.

As the siren sounded at 8.17 that evening, hundreds of people ran from the darkened streets to Bethnal Green Tube Station where some 500 people were already sheltering. Within minutes 1,500 people had entered the shelter. Ten minutes later loud noises nearby panicked many of those who were still trying to enter the station. There was pushing, shoving and then a surge forward. The scene was absolute chaos, certainly not helped by the dimly lit and wet staircase. A woman near the bottom of the staircase slipped, leaving others to fall over, and within seconds over 300 men, women and children were crushed into the tiny stairwell. Rescuers found it almost impossible to help, and eyewitness accounts described the awful 'screaming and hollering' as people were 'piled up like sardines'. The panic had been caused by a salvo of rockets fired a quarter of mile away at Victoria Park by an experimental new

Plaque at Bethnal Green. In spite of efforts at the time to surround this disaster within a wall of secrecy, virtually everyone in London knew it had happened.

Entrance to Bethnal Green Tube Station; the scene of the mass fatalities.

weapon, not by German bombs. The authorities had 'forgotten' to warn local people that these trials were going to take place. At the time the Ministry of Defence placed an embargo on any publicity and did not release information about the incident until 1946.

Years later there were reports of noises similar to those of women and children screaming. In 1981 a station foreman was working late at Bethnal Green Station. He had seen to the usual tasks of securing the station and doing the paperwork when he heard the low sound of voices. As he stopped what he was doing the sound became more and more distinctive. It was the noise of children crying but it gradually grew louder and was then joined by the sound of women screaming. This went on for some ten to fifteen minutes until, overcome with fear, he left his office.

A plaque dedicated to those who lost their lives can be seen above the entrance to the station and a further monument is in the process of being erected.

BRITISH MUSEUM

The British Museum Station, which has long been a disused 'ghost' station, was located on Bury Place near to the museum and was opened in July 1900 by the Central London Railway to service what came to be known as the Central Line. With Holborn Station (opened in 1906) less than 100 yards away, it was decided in 1933 to combine the two stations, and the platforms at British Museum Station were taken out of service. During the Second World War the platforms were bricked up to protect those sheltering from passing trains, though it would appear that these walls were later removed. British Museum Station was used as a military administrative office and emergency command post up to the 1960s. In 1989 redevelopment of the area saw the demolition of the station at street level.

Just before its closure a rumour was circulated that the ghost of an ancient Egyptian haunted the station dressed in a loincloth and headdress. He would emerge late at night and walk along the disused platform wailing as he went. It was said the he was in search of a mummy, possibly a lost princess. As the story grew it caught the attention of a national newspaper who offered a cash reward for anyone who would dare spend a night in the station, although no one took up the challenge.

The ghost story was related to the curse of Amen-Ra's tomb. Princess Amen-Ra, known as the 'Unlucky Mummy' because of the disasters associated with it, died in 1050 BC. The coffin of the Egyptian princess arrived at the British Museum in 1889 and the label on the lid read 'Painted wooden mummy-board of an unidentified woman'. It should be noted that the British Museum claim that they only ever had the coffin lid, not the mummy.

However, the plot thickens. As the *Titanic* crossed the Atlantic in April 1912 the English journalist and passenger William T. Stead told a ghost story about an Egyptian mummy and the translation of an inscription on the mummy's case. The inscription warned that anyone reciting it would meet a violent death. Worse still, the mummy was on the *Titanic* because it had been sold to an American archaeologist who arranged for its removal to New York. The story that circulated was that seven of the eight men who heard the story, and Stead himself as narrator, went down with the ship.

By 1980 the *Washington Post* (17 August 1980) made reference to it when attempts were being made to salvage remains of the *Titanic*: 'Some hunters have spoken darkly of the famous mummy that was allegedly on board, saying it transferred the curse of all who disturbed its grave to the vessel's maiden voyage and to all search efforts.'

The 1933 film *Bulldog Jack* added to the myth that the British Museum Station was haunted by an Egyptian ghost. The film, a comedy thriller starring Ralph Richardson, Fay Wray and Jack Hulbert, involved a plan to steal a valuable necklace, but this all went wrong once the robbers were in the British Museum. The film climaxes in an exciting chase on a runaway train in the London Underground, which also features a secret passage leading into a sarcophagus in the museum.

The idea of an Egyptian ghost dressed in loincloth and headdress looking for a (dubious) mummy on the platform of a station somewhat stretches the imagination. Nonetheless, it is testimony to the power of the press to generate a good, but fictitious, story – something the press has long been very adept at doing.

COVENT GARDEN

Covent Garden Underground Station was opened on 11 April 1907 and is now on the Piccadilly Line. The platforms are accessed primarily by lift (an important point in relation to a ghostly experience which took place here). Moves are afoot (in 2009) to redevelop parts of the station to cope with the heavy use of commuters and tourists.

Covent Garden had a popular and influential minister in the Revd Dr John Cumming (1807–81) who spent much of his time preaching prophecies about the end of the world. In 1860 he commented that, '…the forthcoming end of the world will be hastened by the construction of underground railways burrowing into infernal regions and thereby disturbing the Devil.'

The area has a long association with the theatre and the oldest of these is the Theatre Royal in Drury Lane. It was this association that provided one of the most famous ghosts of the Underground, that of actor William Terriss (1847–97). Terriss, whose real name was William Charles James Lewin, was a popular leading actor of melodramas as well as being a dapper and fashionable man known for sporting trademark white gloves and a cape. Despite him being the darling of audiences he clearly had enemies who envied his success. One particular enemy was Richard Archer Prince, jealous of the recognition that Terriss was getting.

Prince was a struggling actor who had become increasingly mentally unstable and had acquired the nickname 'Mad Archer'. The last straw came on 16 December 1897 when Prince received a letter from the Actors Benevolent Fund (ABF) stating that they were ending the allowance they had been giving him. In his anger Prince went to the Adelphi Theatre where he knew Terriss had his own private entrance and waited for him to turn up for the evening performance. As Terriss entered, Prince ran towards him and stabbed him three times with a knife. A crowd quickly pounced on Prince whilst a doctor attended to Terriss, but the actor died a few minutes later. Prince had some-how convinced himself that Terriss had been responsible for the ending of the money he had received from the fund. A plaque on the wall by the stage door of the Adelphi Theatre commemorates Terriss. At his trial on 13 January 1898 the jury declared Prince to be guilty but not responsible for his actions, and he was sent to Broadmoor.

The ghost of Terriss reputedly haunts both the Adelphi Theatre and Covent Garden Station. Many staff at the station have reported incidents after it has been closed to passengers at night with the ghost manifesting itself in a number of ways. The sound of disembodied gasps and sighs, knockings in the lift and sightings of a ghost-like image of a man were some of the manifestations. Peter Underwood, probably Britain's leading authority and writer on the paranormal, recorded in his book, *Haunted London* (1975), an account told to him by an Underground ticket collector, Jack Hayden. On a cold November night in 1955 after the last train had gone Jack was lock-ing the gates when he suddenly saw a tall, distinguished man with a very sad face and sunken cheeks ascending the emergency stairs towards him. When Jack realised the man might be locked in, he shouted to him to wait and he would let him out. However, by the time Jack undid the gate the man was nowhere to be seen. Four days later Jack saw the man again wearing an old-fashioned grey suit and some light-coloured gloves. Jack asked the figure if he needed the cloakroom but he did not answer and just moved away and disappeared within seconds. Understandably Jack was reluctant to tell anyone of his experience for fear of ridicule. It was only another few days after the second sighting that Jack and one of the guards heard a screaming noise with no one apparently around to make it.

Jack described the ghost to an artist who drew an image of the man which was then passed on to *Psychic News*. They in turn looked through photographs which they showed Jack, who recognised the man he saw in the Underground. It was William Terriss. This story is also born out by a similar experience to

Covent Garden Station opened in 1907 and has a typical Leslie Green-designed frontage. The distance between here and Leicester Square Tube is the shortest between any two stations on London's underground system.

Has the ghost of William Terriss finally decided to rest forever?

that in a Channel 5 documentary, *Ghosts of the Underground* (2006). Another ex-Underground worker, a lift operator, described seeing a tall man in old-fashioned clothes in 1972. Like Jack Hayden, when he was shown a photograph of William Terriss, he instantly recognised it as the man he had seen.

There have been no reported sightings of the ghost of Wiliam Terriss since. From the 1960s traffic congestion had become a huge problem and the area was threatened with major redevelopment, but a public outcry pressured the Home Secretary, Robert Carr, in 1973 to give listed building status to many of the surrounding buildings. It may be that William's ghost came to rest but as changes to develop the station are due to take place it may provoke the ghost of Terriss into a new burst of activity.

FARRINGDON

Farringdon Station is located close to Smithfield Market and is famously haunted by the ghost of thirteen-year-old Anne Naylor, who was brutally murdered in the eighteenth century. The station was opened in January 1863 as the terminus for the original Metropolitan Railway from Bishop's Road, Paddington – the world's first underground railway. This area has witnessed tournaments, duels, the huge Smithfield meat market nearby, the debauchery and rowdiness of Bartholomew Fair (1133–1855) and executions, both hang-ings and burnings. It is also the site of a plague pit. Smithfield is one of London's most historic districts, but seems relatively unvisited by tourists.

In 1758 Anne Naylor and her sister, along with five other girls from parish workhouses, were apprenticed as milliners to Sarah Metyard and her daughter, Sarah Morgan Metyard. Anne was described as being of a sickly disposition and found the work difficult and could not keep up with the other girls. She was singled out by the evil Sarah Metyard and daughter who punished her with barbaric and repeated acts of cruelty, made all the worse when she tried to escape. Some of the other girls saw Anne's body tied with cord and hanging from the door. They cried out to the sadistic women to help her but Anne only received more beatings with a stick and hearth brooms. Poor Anne was locked up alone, bruised, exhausted and starved, and within a few days she died. Her body was carried into the garret and locked up in a box where it was kept for upwards of two months, until it had putrefied and was crawling with maggots.

Eventually the mother removed the body, tried to cut it into pieces and then carried it to what is now Charterhouse Street – close to Farringdon Station. She was unable to get rid of the body parts and she dumped them in the grate of a sewer. The remains were later discovered by a night-watchman who reported it to the 'constable of the night'.

Four years had passed after Anne's murder and it seemed that she would be denied retribution and justice for her brutal murder. It was, however, the continual disagreements between the mother and daughter which proved to be their downfall. The young Sarah Metyard wrote a letter to the overseers of Tottenham Parish informing them about the murder and both mother and daughter were subsequently arrested. The Metyards were also indicted for the wilful murder of Mary Naylor, Anne's sister, aged eight years.

Both mother and daughter were sentenced to be executed at Tyburn (near to where Marble Arch now stands) and then taken to the Surgeon's Hall to be dissected in public, a form of aggravated punishment. On Monday 19 July they were led from Newgate Prison in a cart on the two-mile journey to Tyburn. The mother was described as being in a fit during the journey and left 'this life in a state of insensibility'. As for her daughter, she wept incessantly from leaving Newgate until the moment of her death on the scaffold. After the execution both were 'conveyed in a hearse to Surgeons' Hall, where they were exposed to the curiosity of the public, and then dissected.'

One would like to believe that Anne Naylor found peace but it appears her tormented soul wanders Farringdon Station where she has been nicknamed the 'Screaming Spectre'. Over the years there have been regular reports of the ghost of Anne, the sound of her screams echoing down the platform, and passengers claiming to hear the screaming of a young girl as the last train leaves the station at night.

Farringdon frontage. This is a very historic station, being the city-end of the world's first underground railway. The building here dates from 1923.

Commuters and others claim to have witnessed a ghost in Farringdon Station's passages and platforms.

The boarded-up and inconspicuous entrance to the Highgate Tunnel on the former Alexandra Palace branch.

The 'Ally Pally' Branch. This footpath was fashioned out of the old Great Northern Railway branch line to Alexandra Palace. This is a spooky place on a dark night. No wonder ghost trains are heard.

JUBILEE LINE

From the start the building of the Underground has frequently disrupted old burial sites. In more recent times one such disruption has been that of the Cross Bones burial ground at Redcross Way, between London Bridge Station and Borough Station. The burial ground was excavated by archaeologists between 1991 and 1998 as a result of the extension to the Jubilee Line.

The Cross Bones graveyard lies behind a vacant plot of land enclosed by London Underground boards. Building work in the 1920s led to the exhumation of many bones, as did work in the 1990s for a new substation for the Jubilee Line. The medieval burial ground provided a final resting place for the poor of St Saviour's Parish in Southwark.

The area around was well known for its 'stews', or brothels, and London historian John Stow (1525–1605) wrote in 1603 that the graveyard was used for 'single women' – prostitutes referred to at the time as 'Winchester Geese' because they lived in and operated from dwellings owned by the Bishop of Winchester. By the nineteenth century the area was overcrowded and disease-infested as well as a popular haunt for criminals. Not surprisingly many paupers were interred in the burial ground. It was closed in 1853 because it was not only overcrowded but also a threat to public health.

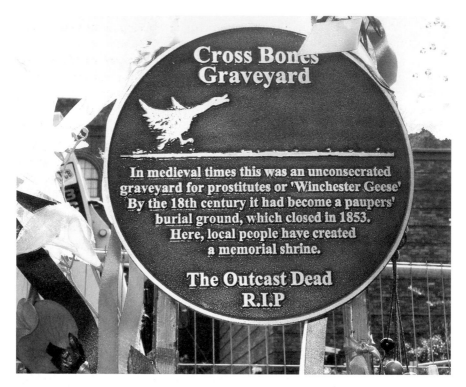

Cross Bones Graveyard.

As more sites are disturbed increased sightings of ghosts are reported; particularly accounts of phantom monks walking the tracks have begun to emerge. However, attempts are made to respect the remains of the dead in such burial sites. For example, Southwark Council was refused planning permission in 2002 for three office blocks to be erected on the graveyard, and future plans hold out the hope that an area will be reserved to serve as a Cross Bones memorial park.

KENNINGTON

Kennington, which opened in 1890, was an intermediate station on the City & South London Railway, the world's first electric tube railway. A feature of Kennington which is little-known to the travelling public is the Kennington Loop. This was built as a means of ensuring that the paths of trains on both the southbound routes of the Northern Line do not conflict where they come together at Kennington. After ensuring that all passengers have been detrained, the drivers of the terminating trains then advance into the single-line tunnel which plunges under the Morden route and then literally loops back on itself so that northbound Charing Cross line trains are now facing in the right direction without having caused any conflicting traffic movements.

Most train crew do not like the Loop. Its sharp curves mean that the wheels emit a loud and irksome flange-squeal accentuated by the narrow confines of the tube. More sinister, however, are the frequent reports from train crews about the threatening atmosphere in the Loop. Although passengers are never allowed to travel round the Loop, the men and women working trains along this piece of line are sometimes seriously disconcerted by not always being sure they are alone. The worst place for mysterious sounds and an evil atmosphere is when the empty trains are standing at the signal awaiting clearance to enter the Charing Cross platform. Tube trains are, of course, one-person operated, but a number of drivers who have followed procedure and ensured that all passengers have alighted at the southbound side platform, have heard the sound of doors between the carriages being opened and closed while their trains were waiting at the signals to enter the Charing Cross platform. Who or what opened and closed these doors?

The line from the Charing Cross direction disappearing into the Kennington Loop.

Stockwell. This may look like any other tube station but what secrets lurk in the tunnel on the left?

LIVERPOOL STREET

The first underground trains began running from Liverpool Street Station in 1875. The station stands on the site of the Bethlehem Royal Hospital which was founded in 1247 as the Priory of St Mary Bethlehem. In 1676 the hospital moved to a site close by at Moorfields and it began to be known as 'Bedlam'. It made a lot of money from allowing paying visitors to watch the antics of the inmates and to egg them on to perform obscene and repulsive acts, all of which the patrons found highly diverting.

The station precincts are supposedly haunted by the screams of a woman said to have been incarcerated in Bedlam in the 1780s although by this time the hospital had of course moved to Moorfields. Apparently this woman maintained a vice-like grip on a small coin despite every attempt that people made to persuade her to give it up. However, when she died some mean-minded member of staff stole it and she was therefore buried without her talisman. The screams are those of this former inmate whose ghost is presumably looking for the coin or trying to settle accounts with the person who stole it.

LONDON ROAD DEPOT

Few of the travelling public know of the existence of the London Road Depot of the Bakerloo Line. It stands near to St George's Circus in the Lambeth district south of the Thames. It is hidden away from prying eyes below street level but is open to the elements. The depot remains in use for stabling rolling stock.

Bakerloo Line staff have provided many reports of strange noises and unexplained appearances around the depot and most especially in the connecting tunnel. In the sidings in the small hours of the morning repeated metallic-sounding tapping noises have been heard as if an old-fashioned wheel-tapper was at work. This has happened on innumerable occasions at times when no maintenance work was being done on the rolling stock. More disturbing have been the shadowy figures seen passing hither and thither in the sidings, often disappearing into the entrance tunnel. Witnesses have never managed to get a good look at them – the apparitions keep their distance and have been described as 'blurred round the edges'. The appearance of these figures is apparently more disconcerting and puzzling than actually menacing. Was there a burial pit in the vicinity which was disturbed when the Bakerloo Line was built?

Another apparition in the area is that of a nun. She is thought to have been connected with a nearby convent school.

MARBLE ARCH

Marble Arch on the deep-level tube Central London Railway opened on 30 July 1900. Marble Arch stands close to the spot where at least 50,000 people met their deaths between the twelfth century and 1783. This was Tyburn, London's main place of public execution.

One of the station name boards at platform level. The last time any change was made to this familiar design, seen all over the underground system, was in 1972.

There is talk of a mysterious figure at Marble Arch who rides up – nevei down – the escalator. In 1973 a lady passenger alighted at platform level and then made her way towards the exit. It was a quiet time of the day and she was the last person to alight from the train and the last onto the escalator. Letting the escalator move her, she was nearly at the top when she became uneasy, aware of a figure that had noiselessly stolen up right behind her. Not liking to turn her head round completely, out of the corner of her eye she saw what she described as a man, all in black, with a trilby and long, expensive-looking overcoat. His presence so close behind her was menacing. She looked ahead again as she moved off the escalator but then, succumbing to the need to satisfy her curiosity, she turned round again for a proper look. The figure had vanished! As she plunged into the comforting mêlée of people outside the station in Oxford Street she knew someone or something had been there, but she was left wondering where it had come from and where it had gone.

Other users of the Central Line have had a similar experience at Marble Arch – always at times when the station is fairly quiet.

MOORGATE

In 1415 the wall of the City of London was pierced to make the Moor Gate, but the gate was eventually demolished in 1762. The first trains started running to a station in Moorgate in 1865 when the Metropolitan Railway was extended from what is now Farringdon. The Northern City Line part of the station was the scene of the worst ever accident involving a train on London's Underground. The reason why the disaster occurred has never been satisfactorily established.

Just after a quarter to nine on the morning of 28 February 1975, a southbound train entered the terminal platform No.9 without showing any signs of decelerating, and it crashed at about 40mph into a thick concrete wall. A massive rescue and recovery operation was launched, working in appallingly hot and confined conditions. It took over four days to bring all the bodies out. Forty-three people died. Seventy-four were seriously injured.

The driver was an experienced, conscientious and reliable man. Eyewitnesses seconds before the crash said that they had seen him in his cab, upright and looking fixedly ahead, apparently unaware of the wall of death towards which he was careering in such a headlong fashion. The verdict was

The platform now served by suburban trains operated by First Capital Connect which witnessed the horrors of the Moorgate disaster.

accidental death. The mysteries surrounding this appalling catastrophe led some people to seek a paranormal explanation. Did the driver see an apparition? It was probably inevitable that people would appear announcing that they had seen ghosts in this part of Moorgate Station. Others declared that the station had a history of hauntings and strange apparitions. Certainly during the winter of 1974–75, shortly before the disaster, a gang of engineers on the night shift in the Northern City tunnels at the approach to Moorgate saw a figure in blue overalls approaching them. As it got nearer they saw that his face bore a look of appalled horror, but before they could see him too closely, he vanished. All were unanimous in stating that they thought it was the apparition of a line maintenance worker who had been run down and killed by a train on this stretch of line some time earlier. Some believed the disaster was caused by this apparition which had startled and distracted the driver. Others said that the ghost the men had seen earlier was a premonition of the impending disaster.

VAUXHALL

The Victoria Line was a long time coming. Most of the line opened in March 1969 and the extension south to Brixton on which Vauxhall is located opened in 1971.

While the line was being built, a mysterious figure described as being at least 7ft tall, wearing brown overalls and a cloth cap, was seen on a number of occasions in the workings. At that height he was bound to be a bit scary, but he never allowed any of the bolder building workers to get too close to him. This ghost became eminent enough to have an article devoted to him in an edition of *The People* in December 1968. No conclusions were ever reached about who or what he was or what he was doing down there.

CLOSED RAILWAY STATIONS

The mainline railway network of Greater London is one of extraordinary complexity. However, compared to the system in the provinces, London's railways have escaped relatively unscathed from the welter of line and station closures which began during the First World War, continuing intermittently through the 1950s and then surging in the 1960s and '70s, only to become thankfully much more intermittent since that time.

There is something poignant about stations on which the lights have gone out forever. It is easy for us to imagine that the men and women who worked in these places, the passengers that went to and fro and perhaps even the trains themselves return in spectral form to the places with which they were once so familiar.

There are a myriad such sites in London. A few suggestions might include the Seven Sisters to Palace Gates branch of the Great Eastern Railway, the branch from Nunhead to Greenwich Park, traces of the London, Chatham and Dover line from Nunhead to Crystal Palace High Level, the mothballed line between Epping and Ongar or the London & North Western Railway's branch line from Harrow and Wealdstone to Stanmore Village. We can be sure that these and many similar places have their ghosts!

CRYSTAL PALACE

The district around Crystal Palace did have an underground railway of sorts, and a particularly interesting one. There have been reported sightings of ghosts associated with this railway.

The Great Exhibition was held in Hyde Park in London in 1851. It was considered an enormous success at the time and unexpectedly large numbers

The 'ghost' tram lines emerging into Kingsway from the old tram tunnel. It is well over fifty years since trams ran along these tracks.

of visitors flocked from all parts of Britain and many overseas places in order to enjoy the spectacle. Londoners and others took the Crystal Palace to their hearts and wanted it to stay in Hyde Park as a permanent fixture. However, this was impossible under the terms governing the staging of the exhibition and it was quickly dismantled when the exhibition closed. An enlarged version of the building was located at Sydenham Hill and the district round about quickly came to be known as 'Crystal Palace'.

In 1864, about ten years after the relocation of the Crystal Palace, an experimental demonstration 'pneumatic' railway was built in the grounds. A passenger carriage ran on a broad-gauge track for a distance of 600 yards through a tunnel, quickly and silently. A return fare, expensive at 6*d* a time, proved no deterrent to those who wanted to sample this novel form of propulsion. The success of this small-scale operation encouraged a company to propose what would have been London's first tube railway, one that would have run under the Thames. However, it was abandoned because of the financial crisis of 1866. The stub of this tunnel is apparently still in situ.

A few years after its closure a myth developed that the carriage remained within the bricked-up tunnel at Crystal Palace and contained a grisly cargo of skeletal forgotten passengers. These physical human remains may have been unable to do anything about their predicament but their accompanying spirits were apparently highly indignant about being immured in this way and were waiting to exact revenge from the living. Traces of this tunnel could be seen for many years and in the early 1990s an edition of the *New Civil Engineer* carried an article with photographs taken many years earlier inside the tunnel. No abandoned carriage containing equally abandoned skeletons was to be seen, and if there were ghosts they chose not to manifest themselves. According to the article, no trace of the tunnel still survived. This has not prevented occasional reports of spectres in the vicinity.

DEFUNCT UNDERGROUND
STATIONS

Between one and about five in the morning, the Underground system is closed and the current is switched off allowing an army of maintenance workers to patrol, check, fix and mend, to ensure that the next day's services will be punctual and safe.

The unmistakeable frontage of the closed station in Kentish Town Road.

How spooky and atmospheric the labyrinth of tunnels, platforms, stairways, passages, sidings and shunting necks that make up the system must be when not in use. What lurks down there in the dark? Plenty of rats, for sure, but are there other entities, living and some perhaps deceased, that become active when the last passengers have been excluded for the night? Many stations have tunnels and passages that are sealed off from public use. What is behind those doors?

At least the active stations come back to life in the morning to serve the needs of the capital but there are many stations on the underground system that have lain dormant for many years. Among former stations with substantial remaining evidence at street level are Aldwych, York Road, South Kentish Town and Brompton Road. Just visible from passing trains are parts of such stations as St Mary's (Whitechapel Road), York Road, British Museum and City Road. Passengers may catch glimpses of some abandoned stations as the train passes through them. At least two stations have ghostly associations, Aldwych and British Museum, whilst South Kentish Town is the subject of an atmospheric and creepy short story by Sir John Betjeman (1906–84).

'GHOST' STEAM TRAINS

The ending of mainline steam trains on British Railways in 1968 received extensive coverage in the media of the time, but no sooner had this happened than stories started circulating that there were ghost trains on the London Underground! Steam-hauled passenger trains on the Metropolitan Line had ended in 1961 but London Transport had long used a small fleet of

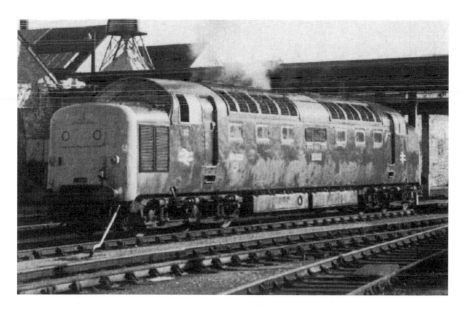

Deltic-class locomotive. The ghost of a locomotive of this class, No. 55020 *Nimbus*, is said to haunt Hadley Wood Tunnel to the north of London on the East Coast Main Line.

steam locomotives on engineers' and various other departments' trains on the sub-surface lines. There had always been something rather mysterious and surreptitious about these trains which mainly ran at night, and the unmistakeable sound and smell of steam locomotives at work in the witching hours began to create a new piece of London folklore. Ghostly steam trains were at large on the Underground!

Since the 1970s there have been occasional reports of a ghostly steam locomotive which manifests itself on the Northern Line between East Finchley Station and the nearby Wellington Sidings. The stretch of line between Gipsy Hill and Crystal Palace is very hilly and between the two stations the line runs through Crystal Palace Tunnel. This tunnel is reputed to be haunted. Many years ago a track maintenance worker was run down and killed by a train in the tunnel. He was decapitated in the process. His ghost has been seen on many occasions wandering disconsolately around the tunnel apparently engaged in the search for his missing head.

Hadley Wood Station is a semi-rural suburban station in a cutting between tunnels on the line out of Kings Cross. For long the double track through Hadley Wood had been a considerable bottleneck, and eventually in 1959 the line at this point was quadrupled. The tunnels go by the simple names of Hadley Wood North and Hadley Wood South. Some people believe that Hadley Wood South Tunnel is haunted by a ghostly diesel locomotive. This is D9020, later known as No.55020, one of the famed 'Deltic'-class, named *Nimbus* after a classic racehorse.

ROAD SIGNS TO
GHOST STATIONS

Road signs only started to become common in the late nineteenth and early twentieth century. Since time immemorial, with the horse being the prime mover, milestones had been used to provide information about direction and distances, and signposts giving such information were rare. On the turnpikes established in the eighteenth and early nineteenth centuries, milestones were obligatory. From the 1900s, however, the widening use of motor vehicles with their higher speeds required a new and different marker from the old established milestone. The earliest fingerpost sign is almost certainly that standing at the meeting place of the A44 and B4081 roads near Broadway Hill in Gloucestershire. On it is the date 1669.

These signposts came in varied styles, often designed and manufactured locally, and they could be very distinctive to the local authority which erected them. Examples are those put up by the old West Riding of Yorkshire County Council. Uniquely, perhaps, and even rather eccentrically, their signs gave the grid reference of the location of the sign itself as well as the name of the place. With road traffic inexorably rising in volume, standardised and supposedly simpler and more visible signs have increasingly replaced the old, idiosyncratic signs. Where old ones can still found, they are frequently off the beaten track.

Railways came to play an extremely important role in the life of both town and country in the nineteenth century and have continued to do so in lesser or at least different ways since then. Many passenger and goods stations and, of course, whole lines have been closed and virtually all traces of their existence obliterated. Sometimes only a superannuated sign can provide a clue to the whereabouts of an erstwhile station. Here we list a few examples of such anachronisms. These all made it into the late twentieth century but we cannot guarantee that they all remain in situ at the time of writing. We like to think of them as signs to ghost stations.

BALNAGUARD

In a brave but forlorn attempt to attract more business, the LMSR in 1935 opened a basic halt at Balnaguard on the Aberfeldy branch of the former Highland Railway. In the centre of the small village there was, at least as late as 1981, a black and yellow sign indicating a path to the LMSR halt. Only half the sign was still in situ, so it read 'Balna', but the cunning and resourceful traveller could nip round to the other side and read the 'guard' bit, if only for reassurance. It is to be hoped that no naïve traveller has set out along the footpath to the halt in expectation of catching a train. The line closed in 1965.

DRUMMUIR

This sign, still extant in 1989, pointed to the station from the main A920 road through the village. A rectangular sign showed an arrow with the words 'Drummuir Station', and reassured the weary traveller that it was only a quarter of a mile away. Drummuir was on the line of the Great North of Scotland Railway between Keith and Craigellachie which closed completely in May 1968.

DUNMOW

Still informing or perhaps confusing would-be travellers in 1980 was a sign in the small Essex town of Dunmow. One arm of this was unusual for sporting the words 'L.N.E.R. Station & Goods Yard'. Dunmow was an intermediate station on the rural Bishops Stortford to Braintree branch of the Great Eastern Railway, which became part of the LNER. The arm containing the words quoted above seems to have been stolen, probably in the late 1990s. It may well have pride of place in the collection of a reclusive 'enthusiast'. Passenger services ceased at Dunmow in 1952 and goods services followed suit in 1969.

EASSIE

Eassie was a small wayside station on the main line of the former Caledonian Railway between Perth, Forfar and Aberdeen. It closed to passengers in 1956 and to goods in 1966, but the sign was still doing sterling service at least as late as 1991. A little bit of people's art in the medium of iron, it informed those who gazed upon it that Eassie Station was a mere one and three-quarter miles away.

HAROME

In 1999 a sign at a road junction in North Yorkshire was still proudly flaunting the words 'Harome Siding'. This was a mute reminder of the importance of the railway in the rural economy. No passenger facilities were provided at the siding which was a considerable distance from Harome (what a wonderful name!), but doubtless in its time it had been of great use to the farmers of the district. Having gone into raptures about the name Harome, it is only fair to add that the indicator on the same post but pointing in the opposite direction tells the observer that it is only two miles to Wombleton. What about that for a name?

Harome Siding was on the Pickering to Gilling branch of the North Eastern Railway which officially closed in August 1964.

SCORRIER

It was unusual for milestones to be used to provide directions to railway stations, but in 1996 one could be found beside the B3298 road at Scorrier advising that it was half a mile to Scorrier Station. Scorrier was on the main line of the former GWR between Plymouth, Truro and Penzance. It closed completely in the autumn of 1964.

THORINGTON

Boldly providing some succour for any stranger looking for a railway station was a sign in the village of Frating in Essex. This pointed down a country lane to Thorington Station, adding that it was only two miles. This sign was still doing what it was designed to do in 2003 although the station itself had closed for passengers in 1957. The line between Colchester and Clacton on which Thorington was a wayside station is still operational.

THE HAUNTED UNDERGROUND
IN FILM AND TELEVISION

Aclassic BBC TV series was Nigel Kneale's *Quatermass and the Pit*, broadcast in the winter of 1958–59. The main setting for the series was a studio-constructed building site, whereas the film version (1967) was set mainly around a fictional Underground station, 'Hobbs End'. In the film, workers discover what they believe to be an unexploded Second World War bomb near the station platform during the extension of what was supposed to be the Victoria Line. As they gradually begin to uncover the mysterious object it turns out to be a spacecraft, millions of years old, bearing the fossilized bodies of dead aliens. Professor Bernard Quatermass, a brilliant but unconventional scientist, is brought in to shed light on this disturbing discovery which turns out to have unforeseen effects on the local populace. Quatermass discovers that people living in the area have experienced ghostly manifestations and poltergeist outbreaks since the building of 'Hobbs End' Underground station in 1927. In one scene Quatermass looks at two street signs. The older sign is spelt Hob's End. Quatermass is then informed that 'Hob' is an old name for the Devil.

The story weaves all the ingredients of a supernatural story: aliens, superstition, archaeological excavation, possession, haunted houses, science, ghosts and horror. The changing of the location from a building site on the TV series to an Underground station for the film was an inspired one. Construction of the actual Victoria Line was started in the early 1960s, some five years before the film. When the line was extended south of the Thames to Brixton, engineers encountered various problems including the finding of fossils and a number of human remains from an old plague pit. The disruption to the pit soon prompted reports of a ghostly presence haunting the area.

Other TV series with a supernatural element featured on the Underground include *Doctor Who – The Dalek Invasion of the Earth* (1964) which made extensive use of the derelict 'Wood Lane' station; *The Web of Fear* (1968) in which several scenes were shot in the Greenwich Foot Tunnel (although the film-makers mainly used a studio set); *Mysterious Planet* (1986); *Blakes 7: Ultraworld* (1980) and more recently *Primeval* (2007). The *Primeval* episode, as with almost all films featuring the London Underground, was filmed at Aldwych. This closed Underground station has also been the location for spooky films such as *Death Line* (1972), *Ghost Story* (1974), *Creep* (2004) and the TV series *Most Haunted* (September 2002). *Lifeforce* (filmed in 1985 at Chancery Lane) also deals with alien forces taking possession of London, although this time turning the population into zombies.

The most interesting documentary to be made around the theme was *Ghosts of the Underground*, shown on Channel 5 in October 2006. The programme drew on the experience of people who had spent most of their working lives on the Underground. It was a credit to the programme that it did not sensationalise but allowed a number of employees simply to talk about experiences that they had had at work for which there did not seem to be any simple explanation. This rather understated approach brought a real sense of eeriness to the programme while at the same time making the accounts of the witnesses sound very believable.

Neverwhere was a six-part television serial first shown in 1996. Based on the book by Neil Gaiman, it tells the surreal tale of a sinister world known as 'London Below'. Set in modern-day London (London above), the series uses the Underground to reflect an uncongenial city that has been left behind. The central character, Richard Mayhew, an average sort of man, stumbles into the murky world of London Below, which consists of a city of monsters, murderers, monks and angels. Familiar names take on a new significance in London Below. The Angel, Islington, is a real angel, the Black Friars are dark priests, and Old Bailey is a character who wears clothing made of feathers. The closed Down Street Station on the Piccadilly Line, which had been converted for use as a secret command centre during the Second World War, was used for the banquet scene in the serial. The station, which was close to Hyde Park Corner tube station, closed in 1932, but its bulls' blood-red faience tiling is still visible at street level.

TROGLODYTES!

The idea of people or creatures living in the Underground over many years has been the stuff of both urban legend as well as providing inspiration for films. These subterranean species have varied from large mutant rodents, hybrid creatures, to a forgotten troglodytic race whose ranks have been swelled by vagabonds, escaped prisoners, and even people who never returned to the surface during the Blitz. According to *Fortean Times* reporter Michael Goss, these survivors have been reduced 'to near-bestial form... They [allegedly] prowl the sewers and railway tunnels showing themselves as little as possible... They probably eat the sandwiches and burgers we discard and it is "widely believed" that they also eat tramps, drunks and other isolated late-night commuters.' Mass Observation (the social research organisation founded in 1937) reported in April 1943 on a study of tube life among the regular shelterers. They commented that some families had 'established themselves permanently in the shelters, having abandoned their homes altogether. Children almost three years old had never spent a night at home...'

In the British horror film *Creep* (released in 2005) a young woman, Kate, having failed to catch a taxi, heads for the Underground where she waits for a train and promptly falls asleep on a seat (supposedly at Charing Cross). When a train eventually arrives Kate realises she is the only passenger. As the film progresses she meets up with a couple who have made their home in a small room at the station. They tell Kate about a creature creeping around killing homeless people. Kate inevitably encounters the 'creep', a mentally deranged cannibalistic hermit who feeds on strays and workers alone in the Underground. A controversial aside to this was that the poster for the film, which shows the bloody hand of a murdered passenger on an Underground train, was banned from all subway stations because it was deemed 'too gory'.

Death Line (1972, aka *Raw Meat*), starring Donald Pleasance, must have inspired *Creep* as it takes up the theme of a lost tribe of people. These are the descendants of workers (men and women) who were buried by a railway tunnel cave-in in 1895 during the excavation of a line between Holborn and Russell Square. The 'lost tribe' survived and bred for many years. They ate people who ventured alone into the rabbit warren of tunnels. However, only one of the tribe is now alive and he is in search of new victims. When the body of a prominent Ministry of Defence official is found a search begins to uncover a secret enclave of survivors beneath the tunnels.

A scene in the film *American Werewolf in London* (1981) shows an unfortunate commuter getting off a train onto an empty 'Tottenham Court Road' platform. As he makes his way to the exit via the escalator he is stalked by the lurking presence of a werewolf. The man desperately runs to get away from the creature but soon falls prey to it. Another type of mythical creature, a dragon, is released from its long hibernation in *Reign of Fire* (2002), as a result of the building of the 'Docklands Extension Line'. Once free, it breeds at a phenomenal rate, eventually wiping out most of the world by 2024. Other apocalyptic and dystopian-style films have also made use of the Underground, such as *28 Days Later* (2002 – Canary Wharf); *28 Weeks Later* (2007 – the actual exterior of the Jubilee line platform); *Survivors – The Lights of London, parts 1 & 2* (1977); and *Code 46* (2004 – Canary Wharf). The 1999 film *Tube Tales* follows a series of mysterious and funny encounters, based on the true-life experiences of London Underground passengers. One of the nine stories, *Steal Away*, follows two young people escaping from a robbery that they have committed. Using Holborn and Aldwych stations as locations, they try to escape and find themselves on what appears to be a disused station until a mysterious train pulls up and they board. Events soon take the form of a series of ghostly encounters.

THE HAUNTED UNDERGROUND
AND LITERATURE

The London Underground has also provided the setting for many novels and short stories. Clare Clark's dark and gruesome murder story, *The Great Stink* (Viking 2005) is set in the sewers of mid-Victorian London just prior to the building of the London Underground. However, compared with films, fictional stories about supernatural Underground activity are thinner on the ground, which is surprising given the ominous and eerie subterranean setting of parts of the Underground.

One of the first ghost stories set on the Underground was by Sir Thomas Graham Jackson (1835–1924), a leading architect as well as a writer of ghost stories. In *A Romance of the Piccadilly Tube* the central character, George Markham, catches a crowded train at Piccadilly Station where he later witnesses a very grisly accident involving a man he knows who is swept under a passing train.

A commuter nightmare is the theme in the short story by R. Chetwynd-Hayes, *Non-Paying Passengers* (1974) where the main character, Percy Fortesque, sees the ghost of his despised late wife Doris reflected in a train window.

In one of his last ghost stories, *Bad Company* (1956), Walter De La Mare opens with the chilling line, 'It is very seldom that one encounters evil in a human face…' The story opens with the narrator descending to one of London's 'many subterranean railway stations' and describes the eeriness of the platform with its 'glare and glitter, the noise, the very air one breathes affect nerves and spirits'. The story unfolds when the man boards the train and sits next to a cadaverous-looking old man whose appearance makes the narrator recoil in disgust. The haunting figure continues to lure the man to a decrepit London residence in order to reveal a last will and testament.

The Eighth Lamp by Roy Vickers appeared in *The Novel Magazine* in July 1916 – reproduced in *Macabre Railway Stories* (1982) edited by Ronald Holmes.

It opens with the last train of the night on the Underground pulling into a fictitious Cheyne Road Station. We learn that 'Cheyne Road station was wholly underground...and the regulations did not apply to it. There are eight lamps on each platform.' Signalman George Raoul, 'transferred from Baker Street', sets about his work on the deserted station. As he walks past the third lamp on the platform he stops and shudders at the sight of a recruiting poster (the story was written during the First World War) with the 'beckoning smile of a young soldier like a mirthless grin of a death mask'. George convinces himself it was the 'new station that was doing it'. As he continues switching off each of the lamps we are told that George cannot look at a 'Circle train without a faint shudder.' By the time he reaches the fifth switch his nerve begins to falter. As he reaches the seventh lamp he is whistling to himself in order to allay his nerves as well as attempting to humanise the desolation. George finally approaches the eighth lamp and extinguishes it. He then waits within a couple of feet of the staircase, crouching. 'He could not see more than a few feet in front of him, but he could hear, distinct and unmistakable, the rumbling murmur of an approaching train.' Impossible, he thinks, no trains are running, but the sounds grow louder. The train appears but it has no lights and George can see that it is a Circle train. Despite telling people what he saw, it is difficult to convince them that a train was running at that time of night. For George the horror is only just beginning as he has to face the spectral force and the mystery behind it on his next shift.

South Kentish Town is an atmospheric and eerie short story by Sir John Betjeman (1906–84). It concerns a clerk, a regular traveller on the line, who mistakenly gets off a tube train on the Northern Line when the doors accidentally open at a disused station. To the man's horror the train moves off, leaving him all alone on the pitch-black platform. Confused and obviously disorientated, he gropes around and locates the emergency spiral staircase, all 294 steps, up to the old station buildings at street level. As he nears the top he bangs his head on the floorboards of one of the shops where the station concourse used to be. He calls out but no one hears him. Utterly deflated, the man then gropes his way back down the seemingly never-ending staircase to the platform. The terrifying feeling of being trapped and not knowing how to escape from an awful predicament is superbly conveyed. Betjeman's subtly understated tale taps into our fears of the dark and of being alone with untold possibilities of nasty things lurking, particularly in the bowels of this labyrinthine network. There was indeed a South Kentish Town Station on the Northern Line. It opened in 1907 and closed as early as 1924. Its red tiled exterior can still be seen at the junction of Castle Road and Kentish Town Road. It is currently used for commercial purposes.

Betjeman's short story of a lone commuter has provided plenty of material for variations on this theme, although some of these have been much less subtle than *South Kentish Town*. The London Underground has provided a mass of fertile material for literature, film and TV, including many tales of the supernatural. Whilst the terrors of Betjeman's unfortunate clerk were mainly in his own mind, other characterisations set on the Underground have produced more sinister phantoms and creatures that threaten those who dare to be alone.

John Wyndham (1903–69), a well-known science fiction writer whose work included *Day of the Triffids*, wrote a short story called the *Confidence Trick*. It involves a commuter, Henry Baider, who travels by Underground from Bank Station on his way home from the city. As the crowded train travels west, Henry suddenly realises that there are only three people in the carriage. Could they all have alighted at Holborn? The train goes faster and faster and Henry checks his watch. 'Unusual. Nearly half an hour at full bat, without a station? It's absolutely impossible'. A woman pulls the emergency handle but nothing happens. Midnight arrives when the train slows down and stops at a station. 'It was something Avenue', a woman said.' A voice announces, 'All change. End of the line.' As they step onto the platform a horned creature with a tail, holding a trident, meets them. They follow the creature on what has become a train ride to Hell.

The Last Train (1975) by science fiction writer Harry Harrison is set in both the 1970s and the Second World War! The narrator comments, 'I was on the Gloucester Road…and there was the tube entrance in front of me…I knew the station well…Fine bit of Victorian railway architecture…District and Circle Lines, name right up there in eternal ceramic tile.' He enters the station and goes down the 'dark and grim' stairwell, and then realises he must have gone down an exit by mistake. He sees a stationary train and asks, 'Why wasn't the train moving?' There were no crowds waiting for other trains. 'Yet we just stood there and stood there and I looked around and felt this sudden, penetrating chill.' He then notices a man reading a newspaper dated 8 December 1941. Could he be among the ghosts of that time?

London Revenant (2006) by Conrad Williams deals with the drop-outs who haunt the Underground. Among them is the 'Pusher' whose pleasure is to push people under trains as well as torturing people who live above ground. Tobias Hill's *Underground* (Faber, 2000) takes the reader down long-lost tunnels, makeshift passages, locked and forgotten stations in search of a series of macabre murders. In Nicholas Royle's *The Director's Cut* (2000) a psychotic film-maker finds shelter in a disused station in between murdering passengers on the tube.

THE HAUNTED RAILWAY IN FILM AND LITERATURE

The Gothic was a fashionable architectural style in the Victorian period, and this was reflected in many stations and other railway buildings and installations. The style added to the atmosphere and romance of steam and provided an ideal setting for tales of the supernatural. It is surprising then that there have not been more books and films about railway ghosts.

Railway and film have a long historic association. In December 1895 in Paris the first motion picture *L'Arrive d'un Train en Gare*, was shown to the public (albeit to an invited audience). The film by the Lumiere brothers showed a train pulling into a station, and although the theme was simple enough it caused the audience to duck behind their seats for fear that they might be run over! France, Germany and the United States developed the theme of railways and the supernatural more quickly than the UK.

When the Devil Drives (1907) is a British film in which a taxi driver of a four-wheeled cab takes a suburban family to a railway station. Suddenly the cab driver changes into the Devil. As he arrives at the station he then mysteriously vanishes leaving the confused passengers alone with their luggage. As they board the train and settle down the Devil reappears, this time as the train driver, having got rid of the driver and his mate, and embarks on an incredible journey, much to the anguish of his terrified passengers. The train flies high into the sky, along the coast, plunges into an abyss, seemingly about to enter a tunnel, before it changes course at the last second and takes to the air again. The film ends with a close-up of the Devil's manic, laughing face.

Probably the most famous railway ghost story is *The Signalman* by Charles Dickens. It was first published in 1866 in the Christmas edition of *All the Year Round*. Dickens had his own personal experience to draw on for this short story. He was involved in the Staplehurst rail disaster in Kent in June 1865 in which ten passengers were killed and forty injured. The story apparently takes its inspiration from the cavernous entrance to Kilsby Tunnel in Northamptonshire on what was originally the London & Birmingham Railway. Dickens creates an eerie atmosphere with the railway cutting shrouded in gloom and isolation. The story centres on a conscientious signalman who has been haunted by a ghost. Each appearance of the apparition brings with it a tragic accident. The ghost is a harbinger of doom. The signalman meticulously attends to his job controlling the movement of trains in a signal box next to a tunnel on a lonely stretch of line. In the event of any danger on the track a fellow signalman contacts him via telegraph. However, the signalman of the story receives three phantom warnings of danger when his alarm bell rings. Each ring of the bell is marked by the appearance of an apparition at the entrance to the tunnel, which is then followed by a dreadful tragedy. On the first occasion two trains crash in the tunnel.

> Within six hours after the Appearance, the memorable accident on this Line happened, and within ten hours the dead and wounded were brought along through the tunnel over the spot where the figure had stood. A disagreeable shudder crept over me.

The second warning involves the death of a young woman in mysterious circumstances:

> As a train came out of the tunnel, I noticed, at a carriage window on my side, what looked like a confusion of hands and heads, and something waved. I saw it just in time to signal the driver, Stop! He shut off, and put his brake on, but the train drifted past here a hundred and fifty yards or more. I ran after it, and, as I went along, heard terrible screams and cries. A beautiful young lady had died instantaneously in one of the compartments, and was brought in here, and laid down on this floor between us.

Finally the signalman admits that he has seen the spectre several times within the past week, and the final warning is a horrifying premonition of the signalman's own death: 'at the mouth of the tunnel, I saw the appearance of a man, with his left sleeve across his eyes, passionately waving his right arm.'

The story was adapted for BBC television in 1976 with Denholm Elliot ideally cast as the signalman. The adaptation, which was filmed on the Severn Valley Railway, is a faithful following of the story and creates the ghostly atmosphere to good effect.

A successful story, which was adapted to both stage and film, was the *Ghost Train* (1923) written by Arnold Ridley (1896–1984), well known for his role as Private Charles Godfrey in *Dad's Army* between 1968 and '77. He also wrote over thirty plays. *The Ghost Train* was a huge success for over two years

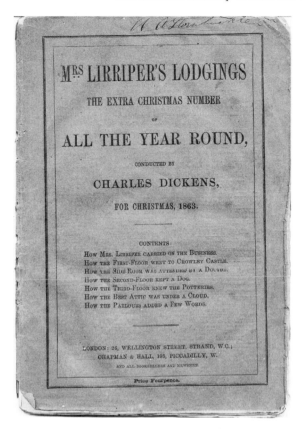

All the Year Round. Cover of the magazine in which Dickens's story, *The Signalman,* was published.

when performed at St Martin's Theatre in London. It was later adapted into film, first in 1931 with the comedian Jack Hulbert and then the well-known version of 1941 starring Arthur Askey, whose antics and humour may have been amusing to some then but are now simply irritating and distract from what is a good story. Ridley's inspiration for writing the play came from stories he had heard about Mangotsfield Station just north of Bristol (long since disused). Some accounts suggest the story was based on his own experience of having found himself all alone on the station one night. The story revolves around a group of passengers who find themselves stranded in the waiting room of an isolated country station. An agitated stationmaster tries to get them to leave because, as he warns them, there is a local legend of a ghost train that dooms all those who see it to a premature death. We discover later that the train is in fact smuggling arms and the story has been concocted to frighten away strangers.

Ridley also wrote a sequel called *The Wrecker* (1924), which is about an engine driver who believes his engine is malevolent. His fears are confirmed in the finale when there is a huge train crash. Gainsborough film studios made a film of the story in 1928 with the crash scene filmed on the Basingstoke & Alton Light Railway.

Gainsborough also did the 1941 remake of *The Ghost Train*. The film was made at Lime Grove Studios because railway stations were unavailable for filming during the war. The film was shot in several locations around Devon and Cornwall. In addition to Askey, it included his straight-man Richard 'Stinker' Murdoch (1907–90) who played Teddy Deakin.

Askey portrayed a music hall entertainer, Tommy Gander, who travels to Cornwall to perform in a show on the seafront. On the journey he loses his hat out of the train window and pulls the communication cord to bring the train to a stop. This short delay means that the passengers miss their connection when the train pulls into Fal Vale Station. The next train is not due until the following morning and Gander is clearly not popular. The stationmaster, Saul Hodgkins, played by Herbert Lomas, tells the stranded passengers they must travel to the nearest town but when he tries to arrange transport the phone line fails. Seemingly unable to move the group on, he tells them the legend as they sit around a fire. Forty-three years ago that very night a train was heading for Fal Vale Station when Ted Holmes, the stationmaster, collapsed and died before he could stop the passenger train hurtling past the station. This led to the death of everyone on the train except the driver, Ben Isaacs. According to the legend the phantom train could still be heard on some nights as it roared past the station – and woe-betide anyone who saw it!

The stationmaster then departed, leaving the passengers to make the most of their wartime rationed meal. As the weather gets stormier and the night draws in, the stationmaster makes a dramatic reappearance by stumbling into the station, collapsing and dying – at exactly the same time as Ted Holmes had all those years ago. Although the film was made nearly seventy years ago it had the potential to be much better, and its atmosphere is not really helped by Askey's style of comedy.

In 1937 the comedy classic *Oh Mr Porter* was released starring Will Hay (1888–1949) as the new stationmaster of a Northern Irish train station at Buggleskelly. Together with his fellow workers, played by Moore Marriott (as Jeremiah Harbottle) and Graham Moffatt (as Albert), they encounter the legend of 'One-Eyed Joe', a ghost who is said to haunt the lonely rustic station. The local postman (Dave O'Toole) takes great pleasure in telling the legend to the new stationmaster:

> Every night when the moon gives light, the ghost of the miller is seen, as he walks the track with a sack on his back, down to the Black Borheen… He haunts the station, he haunts the hill, and the land that lies between.

The legend, as with many other local legends, turns out to be a distraction used by gun-runners to conceal their criminal activities. This was a real tactic used in seaside communities of the past when tales of ghosts coming out at night encouraged people to stay at home while the smugglers went about their business.

A slight variation on the crashed train is *Train of Events* (1949), which attempted, but not very successfully, to follow the stories of three sets of people as they travel on a night train from Euston to Liverpool. Although not specifically a ghost story, there is a sense of impending doom underpinning the tale. The engine driver, played by Jack Warner, says what will be a tragic and inevitable farewell to his wife. The passengers include an actor who has murdered his unfaithful wife, an orphan girl who is in love with a fugitive German prisoner-of-war, and a famous conductor who cannot choose between his wife and a glamorous pianist. Although the doomed train will cruelly resolve the problems of the characters, the audience is left to speculate over who will survive.

A collection of railway ghost stories, both factual and fictional, was brought together in the book *The Ghost Now Standing on Platform One* (1990) edited by Richard Peyton. Although these stories include a number from the United States, the few set in Britain include Charles Dickens' *The Signalman*. Also included is *Journey into Fear*, by Arnold Ridley, which takes place on a branch line station during a journey from London to the Pennines, and bears some similarity to *The Ghost Train*.

Amongst other eminent writers is L.T.C. Rolt (1910–74), engineer and prolific author of many books especially on transport and railways. Lionel Rolt's story, *The Garside Fell Disaster*, is told by an old railwayman who worked on the Carlisle line south of a fictional Highbeck Junction where, 'you could travel the length and breadth of England before you'd find a lonelier place than Garside'. As one might expect with such a railway enthusiast as Rolt, one with an eye for detail, the story is well-informed. It takes the theme of an earlier disaster on the line and is set against an atmosphere of storms, a dark night and unexplained events. As the narrator runs to the signal box he finds a worker, Perce Shaw, whose 'hair was all singled out, his face was as white as that wall.' '"My God!", or "You can't do anything", was all he'd say, over and over again.' What had frightened the man? 'What exactly happened in that tunnel we shall never know', says the narrator. The setting has to be the Settle & Carlisle Railway.

A station waiting room can be a lonely and eerie place when no one else is about, and they have provided the setting for a number of short stories. Robert Aickman (1914–81) was an author of supernatural fiction, and in *The Waiting Room* he conveys to good effect an atmospheric ghost story. His tale concerns a man, Edward Pendlebury, who misses a connection from York to Scarborough because of a late-running train from Kings Cross. He catches a slow 'milk and mail' train and falls asleep, goes past his stop and has to get off six stations further on. He then resigns himself to sleeping in the waiting room. He is horribly aware of his lonely isolation on this remote station where: 'beyond…it was so dark that the edges of the two windows were indistinct.' Pendlebury becomes conscious of a deathly cold and the thickness of the air begins to increase. His loneliness is shattered when the air settles and the room is suddenly full of people. What he does not know at this stage is the waiting room was built on top of a burial ground!

Another waiting room story is *The Kill* by Peter Fleming, Ian Fleming's brother. In this short story two men sit in the cold waiting room on a small railway station in the west of England. Typically, it is foggy and the train is delayed – indefinitely. After a long period of silence the younger of the men senses that there is something strange about the other man in the room. As they eventually begin to converse the young man's initial fears about the stranger are confirmed. A variation on this theme is the story by ghost and horror writer A.M. Burrage (1889–1956); *The Wrong Station*. Two men sit 'in the miserable waiting-room at Ixtable junction…and had not spoken…A dense fog had thrown the train service into utter confusion. It was not at all a cheerful kind of night.'

Lost in the Fog (1916), by J.D. Beresford (1873–1947), starts with the sentence, 'London was smothered in fog', and recounts a man's journey to the Midlands. The journey is thrown into confusion when he winds down the window and cannot distinguish anything familiar in the dim grey mass swirling past. The train draws to a halt. He asks a guard what station this is only to discover he is on the wrong line. 'I felt lonely and pitiable. It was bitterly cold, and the mist was thicker than ever. I could hear no one.' He eventually finds some relative comfort in a waiting room where he meets a man warming his hands by the stove. However, there is something in the man's 'attitude and the tone of his voice…I had a curious sense of touching some terrible reality.' His instincts prove to be right as the man begins to tell him a haunting story.

Sir Andrew Caldecott (1884–1951) was a former governor of Hong Kong (1935–37), but he could also turn his hand to writing a good supernatural story. *Branch Line to Benceston* is a tale of murder, revenge and an uninviting branch line.

In 1866 Charles Collins (1828–73), the younger brother of Wilkie Collins, wrote a short railway ghost story, *Compensation House*, for the Christmas edition of *All Year Round*. The story is about a building at Mugby Junction, 'a dark and gloomy-looking building, [which] had been purchased by this Company for an enlargement of their Goods Station.' The tale involves an old man, Mr Oswald Strange, 'who had recently come to inhabit the house opposite,' and 'is obsessed with the absence of any mirrors in the goods station building.' Mr Strange is certainly strange by name and nature. The narrator soon meets a doctor, also an old friend of Mr Strange, who proceeds to reveal the old man's medical condition. He is 'haunted in the strangest fashion that I ever heard of.' The doctor tells of an incident where he walked into a room and saw Strange:

> It was a great bare room, and so imperfectly lighted by a single candle that it was almost impossible…to see into its great dark corners…There were, moreover, two

ancient chairs and a dressing-table. On this last, stood a large old-fashioned looking-glass with a carved frame…from the moment of my entering that room, the action of my senses and of the faculties of my mind were held fast by the ghastly figure which stood motionless before the looking-glass in the middle of the empty room.

How terrible it was! The weak light of one candle standing on the table shone upon Strange's face, lighting it from below, and throwing (as I now remember) his shadow, vast and black, upon the wall behind him and upon the ceiling overhead. He was leaning rather forward, with his hands upon the table supporting him, and gazing into the glass which stood before him with a horrible fixity. The sweat was on his white face; his rigid features and his pale lips showed in that feeble light were horrible, more than words can tell, to look at. He was so completely stupe-fied and lost, that the noise I had made in knocking and in entering the room was unobserved by him. Not even when I called him loudly by name did he move or did his face change. What a vision of horror.

The story is certainly creepy, but it has less to do with the railway and more to do with Mr Strange's past and that which haunts him. Collins was apparently influenced during his stay at Ewell in 1851 when he had to walk home at night from the railway station. Such were the strange noises and haunting atmosphere of the journey that Collins went into a state of panic.

The Staplehurst accident. Dickens worked among the injured and dying immediately after the accident occurred. The horrors he witnessed affected him strongly and influenced his short story about the signalman and the light by the tunnel.

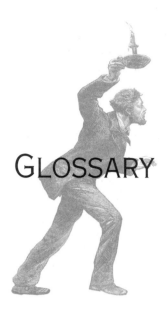

GLOSSARY

In the text, the authors have used some of the words referring to ghostly phenomena in a somewhat loose fashion. They feel that while this is perhaps of no great concern to the general reader, it would be useful to provide a simple listing and definition of some relevant terms.

ANIMAL GHOSTS

Hauntings involving animals account for a maximum of about 5 per cent of reported ghost activity. These reports deal almost exclusively with the types of animal with which humans can have an emotional association and/or those that can be put to some kind of use, e.g. horses, cats and dogs. It is thought that the appearance of some animals in an apparently ghost form may be a portent of the death of the observer. Related to animal ghosts may be reports of supernatural beasts such as black dogs and the numerous alleged sightings of such creatures as big feral cats.

APPARITIONS

Apparitions are the visual appearances of people, animals or things, without their material presence. These manifestations are usually short-lived and they appear, reappear or disappear for reasons that cannot be explained or defined with certainty. Apparitions seem only to be visible to certain people, and, when they disappear, they do not usually leave any physical evidence. They can apparently move through walls, cast shadows or create a reflection in a mirror. Some researchers believe that apparitions are a form of hallucination. 'Collective apparition' is the name given when such a phenomenon is observed by two or more people simultaneously.

CROSSROADS

A long-standing belief in folklore is that crossroads attract paranormal activity. Crossroads were frequently used as the burial place for people who had committed suicide because in former times it was not thought that they should be buried on consecrated ground. To ensure that its spirit did not wander, a stake was driven through the heart of the suicide victim. It was also believed that the conjunction of four roads would confuse the spirit. Crossroad burials at least theoretically ended in 1821 when legislation was passed requiring all church yards to reserve space for the burial of suicides.

CYCLIC GHOSTS

These are ghosts that are believed to manifest themselves regularly on specific dates, especially but not necessarily on the anniversary of their deaths. Vigils organised by investigators on these occasions do not often provide the incontrovertible evidence that they want. In fact, such vigils often involve nothing more than a long, boring and seemingly pointless watch.

The medieval concept of exorcism as depicted in an illuminated manuscript.

DISEMBODIED VOICES

These phenomena involve the sound of human voices without any evident human agency. Many reports of hauntings feature disembodied voices. A common feature of this phenomenon is a warning to the listener – which is ignored at the listener's peril.

EXORCISM

The idea that an individual can be possessed by a spirit, usually a malignant one, which takes control of him or her, is an ancient one. Exorcism is the practice of a ritual, normally performed by a priest, to drive out this spirit or demon. Many religious groups embrace the idea of exorcism and continue to practice it, albeit possibly to a reduced extent, in the face of growing scepticism about religion. Also, many people whose behaviour meant that they were once thought of as being possessed by demons are now diagnosed as suffering from a mental illness.

GHOSTS

In the simplest terms, a ghost is the manifestation to the living of the soul of a deceased human or animal. Some people claim that there are ghosts of inanimate objects such as ships, aircraft and railway trains, especially those hauled by steam locomotives.

In its early years, photography was gleefully seized on by hoaxers and fraudulent mediums to create a stir; to 'prove' the existence of ghosts or to support the case for their own possession of special powers. Even in modern times, purported images of ghostly presences or activities are not generally regarded as providing indisputable evidence. Where researchers accept that deception is not intended, accidental double exposures or technical faults with camera or film are often held responsible. A limited number of well-known photographic images have never been totally explained away either by supporters or sceptics.

The introduction of digital photography in the 1990s provided a wealth of opportunities to create ghostly images for fun or for the purposes of deception, and has only served to make the issue more complicated.

HAUNTING

'Haunting' is a word usually applied to a place in which repeated ghost activity allegedly takes place. The nature of the phenomena may be visual, aural, olfactory, a combination of these or just a 'presence' sensed in some other indefinable way. Hauntings can also involve temperature variations and the unexplained movement of objects. Generally, the impact of these phenomena seems to lessen with time, which suggests that whatever the force or energy that sustains them, it gradually dissipates.

ORBS

These are phenomena which only seem to have come to popular attention with the arrival and now widespread use of digital photography. Orbs appear to be small, often globe-shaped patches of luminosity not visible to the user of the camera when the picture is taken. While it is claimed by some people that orbs are the souls or spirits of the dead, others argue that they are 'pieces' of concentrated psychic energy. Such paranormal explanations are rejected by those who believe that they are simply airborne particles which have been caught in suspension by the camera.

PARANORMAL

Paranormal phenomena are those which cannot be explained within the existing boundaries of knowledge.

PHANTOM

This word is commonly used as a synonym for an apparition. There is a strong sense that a phantom is sinister or threatening.

William Hope, a medium who claimed that he could get in touch with the ghosts of the dear departed.

POLTERGEIST

Many reports of supposedly paranormal activity are ascribed to the presence of poltergeists. The word literally means 'noisy spirit'. Poltergeists are blamed for a wide range of irksome activities including the movement of objects, the throwing of things sometimes apparently with malicious intent, for causing fires, tampering with equipment, physical assaults and mysterious knockings and other sounds. Outbreaks of poltergeist activity are not usually prolonged and those who have investigated such phenomena frequently argue that an individual is unwittingly responsible – usually a person undergoing troubled emotional experiences or a teenager having problems coping with the transition from childhood to adulthood.

RE-ENACTMENT GHOSTS

These are apparitions that seem to re-enact emotionally charged events of the past such as battles, disasters or murders.

REVENANT

This word is sometimes used to refer to a person who returns from the dead, often after a long absence, in the form of a ghost and apparently with the intention of making contact with the living, usually its erstwhile relations or friends. On occasions it is thought that the revenant wants to impart some advice or information to the still-living. It is thought by some that revenants may be the spirits of those who were never properly buried.

SPECTRE

A word used to refer to apparitions and ghosts or, in a loose sense, to their supernatural entities.

SPIRIT

A spirit can be defined as a paranormal, possibly supernatural, being or essence which can manifest itself in a multitude of different guises. Mostly they seem to want to communicate a message or give a warning to the living.

SUPERNATURAL

'Supernatural' differs from paranormal because of the implication that such phenomena are the result of forces beyond human understanding and control.

WRAITH

A wraith is the appearance of a living person which manifests itself as a portent just before or at the actual person's death.

Other titles published by The History Press

Haunted London Underground

David Brandon & Alan Brooke

London's Underground is associated with a multitude of ghostly stories and sightings, particularly on stations and abandoned lines, many of which are in close proximity to burial sites from centuries ago. This chilling book reveals well-known and hitherto unpublished tales of spirits, spectres and other spooky occurrences on one of the oldest railway networks in the world.

The stories of sightings include the ghost of an actress regularly witnessed on Aldywch Station and the 'Black Nun' at Bank Station. Eerie noises, such as the cries of thirteen-year-old Anne Naylor who was murdered in 1758 near to the site of what is now Farringdon Station, and the screams of children who were in an accident at Bethnal Green Station during the Second World War, are still heard echoing. These and many more ghostly accounts are recorded in fascinating detail in this book, which is a must-read for anyone interested in the mysterious and murky history of London's Underground.

ISBN 978-0-7524-4746-9

Haunted London Pubs

David Brandon & Alan Brooke

This book reports the many stories of ghostly sightings at London's drinking places, and delves into the fascinating history surrounding them in an attempt to unearth who and what these phantoms might be. From the ghosts of convicts still trying to escape the nearby Millbank Prison through tunnels under the Morpeth Arms, to the chilling spectre of the screaming girl at The Suchard in Crucifix Lane, this book is a creepy must-read for anyone interested in the haunted history of London's pubs.

ISBN 978-0-7524-4760-5

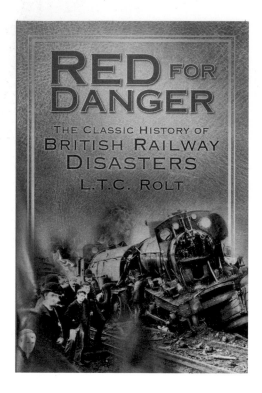

Red for Danger: The Classic History of British Railway Disasters

L.T.C. ROLT

'Railway enthusiasts should consider it essential.'
BOOKS AND BOOKMEN

First published in 1955, and the result of Rolt's careful investigation and study of the verbatim reports and findings by HM Inspectorate of Railways, this book was the first work to record the history of British railway disasters, and it remains the classic account. It covers every major accident on British railways between 1840 and 1957, and the resulting change in railway working practices, and reveals the evolution of safety devices and methods which came to make the British railway carriage one of the safest modes of transport in the world. This edition uses the last text produced by Rolt himself in 1966 and includes a new introduction by his friend and fellow railway historian Professor Jack Simmons.

ISBN 978-0-7524-5106-0

Visit our website and discover thousands of other History Press books.
www.thehistorypress.co.uk